The Designer's Guide to Creating

CORPORATE
I.D. SYSTEMS

Rose DeNeve

Cincinnati, Ohio

96 95 94 93 92   5 4 3 2 1

Library of Congress Cataloging-in-Publication Data

DeNeve, Rose.
      The designer's guide to creating corporate I.D. systems / by Rose DeNeve. —
1st ed.
            p.   cm.
      Includes index.
      ISBN 0-89134-441-1
      1. Corporate image — Graphic methods — Case studies. 2. Commercial art. 3.
Signs and symbols. 4. Graphic arts — Technique. I. Title. II. Title: Corporate I.D.
systems.
      HD59.2.D46   1992
      741.6 — dc20   92-5064
                                                                                         CIP

Edited by Mary Cropper
Designed by Clare Finney

The following page constitutes an extension of this copyright page.

Credits

Acknowledgments

Writing a book as research-intensive as this one calls on the forbearance of an author's colleagues, who contribute their time and expertise, and family, who contribute their patience and support.

In particular, I would like to thank Jack Hough and his colleagues, Henry Goerke and Steve Chapman, for sharing with me their many years' experience as corporate designers. Their day-long discussions provided a real groundwork for this book.

Other people, too, contributed outstandingly with time and effort, as well as information and materials. Many graphic designers graciously supplied their work in graphic identity to be considered for and published in this book, and it would be impossible to thank them sufficiently or individually. However, not a few went to considerable lengths to provide what I was looking for: Sheree Clark, Paul Browning, Karen Mokry, Jeff Larson, Art Chantry, Bart Crosby, Alina Wheeler, Dick Held, Ron Sullivan, Mark Perkins, Linda Helton, John Evans, Kathy Klein, James Skiles, David Butler, Bennett Peji, Wendy Croft, Jill Gabbe, Joel Portugal, and last but by no means least, Lynne Garell.

I would also like to thank certain corporate liaisons for allowing me to include historical perspectives of their company's logomarks: Richard Kerans at Crane & Co.; Judith Fadden and Steven H. Hartman at Nabisco Brands; Paul Rand for IBM; George Schweitzer and Azita Gorton at CBS; Michael Focarile at Citicorp; and William Cohrs and Bill Rawl at Exxon.

Finally, I would like to thank my editors at North Light—Susan Conner, whose early input helped focus the book's content; Perri Weinberg-Schenker, for her conscientious copyediting; and Mary Cropper, who helped me through some difficult development stages, and whose persistent slashing and burning of the manuscript resulted in tighter copy and sharper points. Mary also managed the day-to-day crises of creating the book, and so, in many ways, it is as much hers as it is mine.

To my mother, for her patience and support

Contents

Introduction

In the last several years, there have been many new books about the phenomenon called corporate identity. Some have been collections of trademarks; others have attempted to explain the corporate view of the subject; a few have focused primarily on the history of identity design.

While this volume incorporates some elements that might be found elsewhere, it seeks to add another significant dimension: to speak of graphic identity in terms of its actual application to real businesses, both large and small. Its primary goal is to teach, through words and pictures, the process of graphic identity design in such a way as to make it accessible to all design practitioners, serving any size or type of client.

This book is organized into several sections. One deals with the past — the concept of graphic identity as it has been developed and applied in America. This information is included because the author believes that, like all professionals, graphic designers operate in a continuum, and knowledge of this continuum informs and empowers them. This section concludes with a survey of the basic elements involved in graphic identity design.

But the bulk of this book deals with the hands-on practice of devising corporate identity, for this is where graphic designers live every day. Every step in that process, from initial client contact to the implementation of the identity program, is covered in depth. A generous helping of visual materials from real-life identity programs has also been included to both delight and inform — these illustrations are best considered by the reader within the context of their individual creation, for it is here that the designer will gain insight into both the thinking behind, and the process of, designing corporate identity.

What Is Corporate Identity and Who Needs It?

Back in 1959, William Golden, who created the renowned eye for the CBS network, wrote in *Print* magazine, "A trademark does not in itself constitute a corporate image. . . . [Image] is the total impression a company makes on its public through its products, its policies, its actions, and its advertising effort. I suppose a trademark can serve as a reminder of a corporate image, if you have one."

Golden's words reveal an elementary distinction in the world of graphic design: Image is how you're perceived; identity is who you are. What we call "corporate identity" is the graphic expression of both. As a graphic expression, a company's identity can be created and can influence its destiny.

There is a strong awareness among businesses today of the importance of creating and maintaining a powerful graphic identity. As more and more companies — many producing the same products — compete in a broadening marketplace, a graphic identifier becomes a major distinguishing feature.

Big business's deepened understanding of the inherent power of graphic communication has begun to appear among the ranks of small-business owners as well. Consequently, independent designers, or those who operate smaller studios, have an unprecedented opportunity to develop well-conceived, well-executed identity programs.

At the same time, the designer has an increased responsibility to devise an identity that is both effective and appropriate. It has been said that corporate identity is the glue that holds corporate strategy together: It is who the company is, as well as how it and others see itself. Corporate identity must succeed — or fail — within this do-or-die environment.

Where We've Come From . . .

The earliest forms of "graphic" identity date back to antiquity, when potters marked the bottoms of their wares and herders branded their cattle. The heraldic forms that graced shields and manorial banners among the knights of old were a type of visual identity. Thirteenth-century Britain, in an effort to keep bakers honest, required bread to be marked on the bottom with the baker's seal. Artisans caught using bogus marks, we're told, were nailed to the pillory by their ears.

But it was the rise of industrialization, with its manufactured and packaged goods, that gave us logos and marks as we know them today. The earliest trademarks were used to market individual products; as more products were added under the same brand, those marks came to signify the larger company as well. Enduring trade names such as Kodak, Singer, Heinz and Coca-Cola appeared during this time. Although many of the designs from this era were figurative, few came from the hand of a professional artist or graphic designer.

It wasn't until the 1930s that a significant number of graphic designers became involved in what would be known as corporate identity design.

After World War II, as the United States entered a new age of prosperity, the first design firm devoted to brand and trademark design, Lippincott & Margulies, was established. It turned out trend-setting identity programs for companies such as U.S. Steel and Chrysler Corporation.

During the fifties and sixties, visual identity design reached a fevered pitch. The business slackened somewhat during the social and economic turmoil of the seventies, only to be revived in the eighties in a somewhat-altered form. Now a recognized tool of business planning, visual identity has greater importance than ever.

Derived as it is from a typically American entrepreneurial spirit, visual identity design says, "I want to stand out from the group." This attitude has been critical to the founding and success of many American businesses.

. . . And Where We're Going

The language of business is rife with jargon and buzzwords. In the late 1950s, along with terms such as "group think" and "creativity," "corporate image" was much talked about. Today, the lexicon of corporate identity might include the phrases "corporate culture," "corporate voice," and "value-added." Far from being highlights in a trendy vocabulary, this shift in usage reveals a concurrent shift in the corporate view of visual identity.

Corporate identity is no longer merely "a bug and a logo." If visual identifiers were once seen as cosmetic or decorative elements belonging to the realm of public relations, they are now the children of business strategy, reflecting well-thought-out business plans. As such, they can have far-reaching implications for the companies who develop them.

For better or worse, today's graphic design has as much to do with business strategy as with art and innovation. Still, the most successful designs do not sacrifice the latter on the altar of the former. Rather, they get to the heart of a company's uniqueness and express it across the full range of a company's visual communications.

And this is where corporate culture comes in. Just as American culture helps to define our idea of what America is, so, too, does a company's culture contribute to its identity. "Culture" is all the ways a company behaves: how it treats its employees and its customers; what it says in press releases and to Wall Street; what it makes and sells, and how well; its management structure; its heritage and traditions.

Corporate voice is simply the consistent expression of its culture. It is the means by which management unifies its various public exposures to build a coherent image for the corporation. Corporate voice begins with the corporation knowing itself and what it stands for. Thus, defining the corporation and its goals through a carefully written mission statement is the first step in formulating a corporate identity. When the statement is strong and clear, every act, every communication, contributes to a distinctive corporate image.

Some of the oldest and most familiar corporate symbols date literally to antiquity. The National Biscuit Company adapted a 15th-century printer's mark (left) in 1900, placing it in an eight-sided box (center). It went through a few more revisions before Raymond Loewy Associates turned it into a versatile corner seal in 1952. This familiar mark has recently been updated again (right) by one of Nabisco's own in-house designers. That the double-cross and oval insignia is still in use attests to the timelessness of this design.

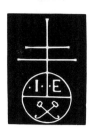

The Esso trademark was one of the earliest designed by a professional designer, namely William O'Neill, who applied it to oil cans and gas stations in the 1930s. The name-and-oval (or circle) identity format remains a favorite to this day.

Designed in 1960 by Chermayeff & Geismar Inc., Chase Manhattan Bank's ground-breaking octagon mark remains one of the best of the early "modern" abstract designs. Its squared-off, interlocking mechanical forms spawned a whole generation of imitators, few of them as successful as the original. Moreover, the "me-too" proliferation of such forms within specific industries renders them fairly useless as distinguishing marks.

Designed by William Golden, the CBS eye first appeared in 1951 as an on-screen identifier and was at the leading edge of the postwar movement toward abstract identity designs. It has been imprinted with the CBS monogram, telescoped inside itself like an image repeated infinitely with mirrors, and even made into the lens of a camera. Never mind. In spite of all these variations, in the forty years since, there have been few marks as instantly recognizable or as successful as pure communication.

Sometime in the 1930s, International Business Machines became known by its initials and adopted them as a monogram. In 1956, four years after the introduction of the company's first vacuum-tube computer, Paul Rand was asked to redesign that logotype. His slab-serif design, he has said, was conceived as a transitional form. A few years later, he added stripes to create additional interest. Since each letterform is a different width, the stripes serve to tie them all together. While stripes as a device have since cropped up in many a logotype, few have done so with such good effect.

Penn's Landing is Philadelphia's most significant riverfront development, a mix of public open space and private commercial, retail, office and residential development. Its symbol needed to be appropriate and dramatic, without competing with the large number of private commercial and retail symbols that would be adjacent to it. Katz Wheeler's task was complicated by the client group's wanting a schooner as part of the symbol, when many of the tenants were already using schooners in their own symbols and signage.

The designers chose to identify the riverfront development as a site, not as a retail operation. The mark incorporates the nautical signal flag for the letter "P" and clearly communicates that Penn's Landing is Philadelphia's square on the water.

Identity Basics

Regardless of appearances, a graphic identity is a complex creature. It encompasses not just a decorative logotype or symbol but also myriad associations, both strategic and emotional. And then, of course, there are the systematic applications of the identity to stationery, signing, vehicles, printed communications and more. It's important for designers of visual identities to have a basic understanding of how these many facets work.

A graphic identity must be conscious of a company's business plan—where the company is now and where it wants to go in the future. An identity developed now must be able to take the company where it wants to go tomorrow, while accurately reflecting who the company is in terms of products, services, and markets, and how its employees feel about working there.

Structure. To effectively communicate, a graphic identity must be conceived within the appropriate structure. Large corporations, for example, need to develop an identity hierarchy that clearly explains—through naming, typography, and graphic identifiers—just what each part does and how it relates to other parts and to the whole. On the other hand, a small business, even one with a few locations, may need only one name and identifier. Its graphic identity would need to describe it, but not necessarily explain it.

There are three principal types of management structure: monolithic, diversified and conglomerate. (In real life, however, you can find any number of variations in between.) Monolithic companies are usually well established in a single business or allied businesses. These companies impart the strength of the whole to the individual operating units. (If you trust mainframe computers made by IBM, then why not IBM PCs?) The diversified company, which has usually grown by moving from a basic business into allied ones, lets each unit feel its own power while sharing the strength of the whole. (Presumably, the forest products division of Continental reinforces the goodwill of the packaging division, and vice versa.) Conglomerates grow largely through acquisition of businesses that may or may not be related. The conglomerate hopes to create a strong identity for itself on the shirttails of its acquisitions. (United Technologies as a whole gains confidence because it owns Sikorsky Aircraft.)

Monolithic companies use a single identifier for all products and services. Diversified companies use a single corporate identifier and add to it a generic product or operating name. Conglomerates impose their corporate identity on that of an acquired company or subsidiary. (A variation on this type of identity occurs when a company such as Procter & Gamble develops a number of different products, each of which has its own name and brand identity.) See the chart on the next page for more on these structures.

Management structures may be communicated with a logotype, with a single symbol, or with several different logotypes and symbols. For example, a highly centralized company ("Joe's Pizza") would use one name, one typeface, one corporate color, and one symbol. As organizational complexity increases, several names and/or typefaces may be used to delineate operating units ("Joe's Pizza," "Joe's Beanery"). In a totally decentralized business, separate names, logotypes and colors might be applied to each unit ("Valley Pizza—A Joe's Company," or "Crystal Cleaners—A Joe's Company"), with the only unifying element being the holding company's symbol or endorsement. (Again, for more on these structures, see the chart on page 8.)

Elements of Identity

The two most common constituents of visual identity are a name and a mark. A company's name is the single most important factor in creating a corporate identity. After the content of the name, the form of the company's visual identifier—be it logotype (using words), mark (symbol) or both—is by far the most important aspect of an identity program. To keep this discussion simple, let's call all such identifiers "logomarks."

Names. A company's good name is the repository of all its equity and goodwill. As more products and services come under its banner, as more money is spent to promote it, and as stock market shares become linked with its content, its importance and value increase. For these reasons—as well as inexplicable emotional attachments—companies are reluctant to change their names.

Company names fall into several broad categories:

• *Founder names.* Many of America's oldest and most venerable companies are named for their founders (Heinz, Campbell's, Gillette). Some are utilized as actual handwritten signatures (Kellogg's, Ford).

• *Descriptive names.* These describe the nature of the company's business. They are easily understood but may be difficult to register if too generic (General Mills, USAir).

• *Coined names.* Although these may be nonsense words, they can be created to specific criteria, e.g., short, memorable, strong, visually interesting (Kodak, Exxon, Textron). But, unless there is some obvious connection to a previous well-known name, new coined names can be difficult and expensive to promote.

• *Associative names.* These may be analogous or purely imaginative (Cat's Paw soles, Wheels auto shops, Jaguar automobiles). Associative names come loaded with personality and are easy to visualize.

• *Abbreviated names.* Those derived from legal corporate names that are less convenient to say (PanAm for Pan American Airlines, NatWest for National Westminster Bank). While they are not necessarily legal names, they are used as primary elements of identity.

• *Initials.* These take over when a corporate name is too long to say easily; after a time, these initials may become the legal name (GE, IBM, RCA). Initial names work when a company has first built equity in the entire name. Most naming experts today feel that, because they lack any intrinsic identity and are expensive to promote, new initial names are best avoided.

Symbols and Marks. Whether signifying companies large or small, well-conceived logomarks are the key to an effective identity program. They identify products and services, differentiating the company and its businesses from

Monolithic companies are usually well established in a single business or allied businesses. They use a single, straightforward identifier for all of their products and services to project a single, unified image to their many audiences. IBM, Xerox and Mobil are well-known large monolithic companies; a smaller one might be a pizza restaurant operating under one name at several locations.

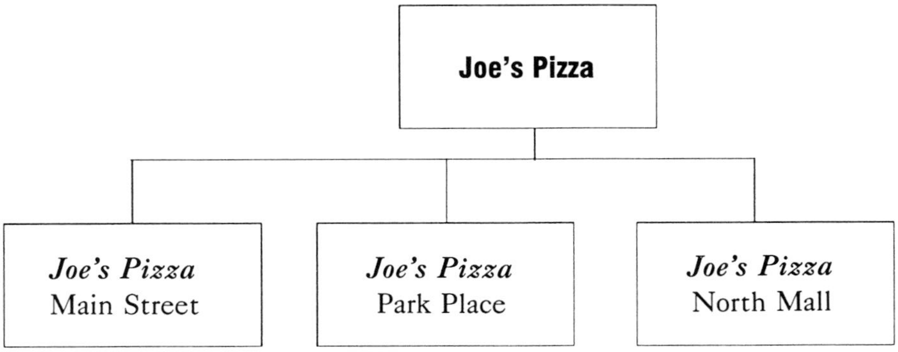

Joe's Pizza

Joe's Pizza Main Street	*Joe's Pizza* Park Place	*Joe's Pizza* North Mall

Diversified companies have usually grown by moving from a basic business into allied ones. These companies most often use a single corporate identifier with a generic product or operating unit name. This allows them to project a cohesive image while at the same time communicating the scope of their businesses. Well-known examples of this type of identity include RCA and Continental Group. A small diversified business might be a restaurateur who started out in pizza but added other types of eateries.

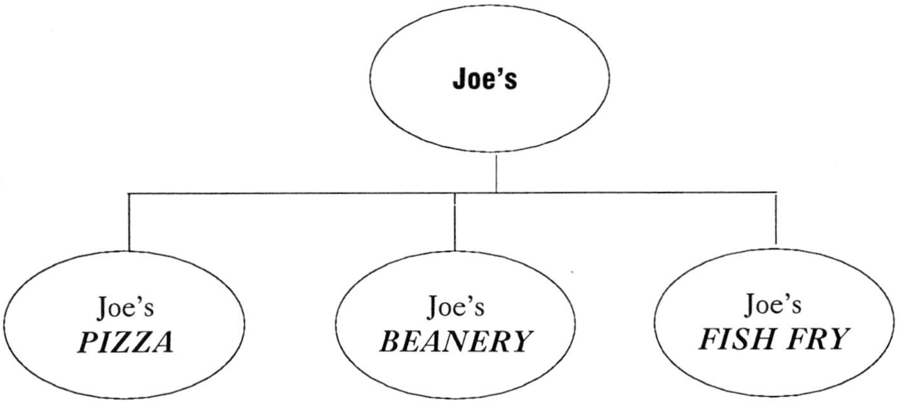

Joe's

Joe's *PIZZA*   Joe's *BEANERY*   Joe's *FISH FRY*

Conglomerates are companies that have grown largely through acquisition of businesses that may or may not be related. Their identities try to reconcile two or more separate business entities with a corporate "endorsement"—the corporate name somehow superimposed on that of the acquired company, or subsidiary. United Technologies is a good example of a large conglomerate identity. A small company might use this form if it operated a number of unrelated businesses.

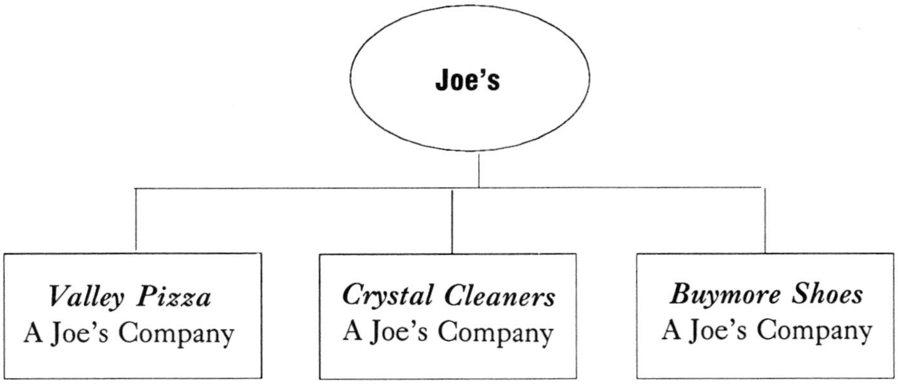

Joe's

Valley Pizza A Joe's Company	*Crystal Cleaners* A Joe's Company	*Buymore Shoes* A Joe's Company

others in the field. They succinctly communicate the company's personality and culture. By serving as an endorsement, they add value to products and services. And they are legal properties that can be controlled and developed over time.

A graphic identity can be a literal signature or pure typography. It can combine the logotype with a geometric form, or it can rely on a graphic symbol alone. That symbol can be a direct depiction of the company name or business, or it can be a pure abstraction with no intrinsic meaning at all.

Much has been written about symbols—about their use and design as well as about their psychological ramifications. Here, it is enough to understand that the most successful reinterpret ordinary things in an extraordinary way. Whether abstract or figurative, the best defy logic and operate on a psychoemotional level, appealing to a wide variety of audiences through shared human values.

Symbols are powerful because, whatever feelings they evoke, the viewer will come to associate those emotions with the entity being symbolized. Obviously, whatever its form, a corporate symbol must be developed very carefully.

Examples of the major types of graphic identifiers are shown on pages 10 and 11. While they have been organized into three main categories, sometimes the distinction among different types is blurred. This is because most graphic identifiers in reality combine elements of more than one type, the advantage being that they gain benefits from each. Combining a logotype with an abstract mark, for example, will add to the mark's recognizability, eventually allowing it to be used without the name. An abstract form imprinted with initials doubles its visual impact and so increases its likelihood of recall. Indeed, in many corporate programs, the standards manual prohibits any use of the corporate symbol without its accompanying logotype.

Symbol Strategies. To be successful, good graphic identifiers must:
- Avoid negative implications.
- Evoke a positive response.

A graphic identity can be pure typography, as shown in this design by Rickabaugh Graphics for Galbraith Hough real estate developers.

LAKELINE MALL

Many logomarks combine type with a geometric or other form, as seen in this design by Sibley/Peteet Design for Lakeline Mall in Austin, Texas.

An identity may rely on a symbol alone. This design was developed from the client's initials by Katz Wheeler for Urban Engineers, a multidisciplinary engineering firm specializing in transportation-related projects. It suggests roads and building elements at different heights.

Typographic marks may use a company's name or its initials, simply put or ensconced in a seal or monogram. The name may be expressed graphically as a signature or as a typographic treatment.

"The Works," a rock group. Larson Design Associates.

KLEC real estate development company, specializing in rehabilitation of troubled, older properties. Bennett Peji Design.

American United Life Insurance Company. Crosby Associates.

Logomark for Harris Sales, toy distributors. Sibley/Peteet Design.

Abstract marks are nonfigurative designs, usually simple and nonrepresentational in form. They are nonspecific and so do not assign any particular attributes to the corporation. Such associations must be built up over time, or "borrowed" from our feelings about similar marks. Originally, abstract marks were used primarily to signify diversified or conglomerate businesses, where a more literal form might be strategically limiting. Now, however, they can signify any business that wants to appear "modern" and "corporate."

Marketing Strategies, a consulting firm that analyzes marketing needs and creates marketing strategies for professional and service sector clients. Katz Wheeler.

The Trails, real estate development. Sullivan Perkins.

Promatch, oil products for Caterpillar. Samata Associates.

Descriptive marks are a more or less literal depiction of the company's name or business. They work best when the company has only one line of business or when they convey the character of the organization, rather than a specific product. If a descriptive mark is too specific, the company may find it difficult to diversify business or product lines under its aegis.

Orrick Herrington & Sutcliffe Child Care Center, a child care center within a law firm. Kiku Obata & Company.

Enders Flowers, a flower shop. Larson Design Associates.

Rockford Recycle, a glass recycling program. Larson Design Associates.

Overland Trading Company. Midnight Oil Studios.

Dallas Uptown, a merchants association. Sullivan Perkins.

• Answer questions of business strategy/planning.

• Meet the company's stylistic and technical needs.

• Be unique unto themselves.

• Be timeless (able to last at least ten to twenty-five years).

• Allow flexibility in applications.

• Be easy and inexpensive to use.

This is not an easy task.

Contemporary symbols have lost a certain utility simply because there are so many of them. One company implements a successful and widely acclaimed identity program; soon its competitors are following suit, often in blatant imitation. The result is a confusion of generic symbols, none of which still meet the criteria to which they were designed.

Because of this trend, many companies are returning to identifiers that are more figurative and more descriptive. These might be cartoon characters, animals, or other identifiable objects, which are coupled with meaningful names. These images are imbued with more personality than yesterday's abstract symbols, and they are usually more flexible in application as well. In the real world, there are few occasions to reduce a corporate mark to one sixteenth of an inch. As one designer puts it, "We don't have to put an angel on the head of a pin."

The Identity System. Beyond the development of the graphic identifier, or logomark, lies a corporate identity's testing ground: its application to the range of materials a company needs to conduct its business every day. Although implementing a systematic identity is perhaps the least glamorous aspect of an identity job, it is one of the most important. If corporate identity is the glue that holds corporate strategy together, consistent implementation of identity is how and where that glue is applied.

Obviously, a large corporation with many divisions and a huge advertising and communications budget is going to require more standards and stricter implementation than a small business with a single location. The important thing to re-

(Above.) Using characters, animals or other identifiable objects as part of a logomark helps the mark stand out in the crowd and gives it some personality, as shown in this design by Sullivan Perkins for Big Annie's restaurant.

(Below.) An identity system may involve more than just stationery and collateral materials. The identity Samata Associates developed for River House, an engraver of fine art prints, was used on banners and signage as well as collateral materials.

R I V E R H O U S E

Any business can use some sort of identity program. Shown here (from top to bottom) are identifiers for Oman & Oman, marriage counselors (Larson Design Associates); W.E. Cleaning, an office cleaning service (Taylor & Browning); and Sue Vanderbilt's Dough Art (Kiku Obata & Company).

member is that, whatever the company's size, consistency pays. Consistent application is how a company's public becomes familiar with its identity, and anything less than consistency spells confusion. Consistency across all of a company's visual communications, whatever their form, is what gives a corporate identity its strength. All else being equal, a company with a strong, well-applied graphic identity will beat its less-well-identified competitors every time.

Who Needs Corporate Identity?

Virtually every business you can think of needs to be well identified. Obviously, the need is greatest when a company is new and has to establish itself in the marketplace against well-entrenched competitors. But sometimes business situations arise where an established, even successful, company considers devising a new graphic identity.

Sometimes an astute management realizes that, to accomplish its business goals, the company has to develop a new idea of itself. A new graphic identity can help it do that. Some fashion-conscious industries, such as retailing, cosmetics and airlines, feel the need to revise their graphic identities every few years. Indeed, some designers think no corporate identity program should be expected to last beyond a decade. There are just too many variables in the business world, and too many changes in the life of a company, for any program to go too long without revision. Whether an existing program should be scrapped entirely or carefully fine-tuned is what the identity process is all about.

But most identity problems arise when the reality of who a company is or wants to be is not accurately conveyed by its graphic identity. Identity and image should be in agreement if the company is to be accurately perceived and is to operate from a position of strength.

The identity problem, then, is one of both management and visualization, or graphics. It is no longer enough to think of the company letterhead, or the name on the door, as an exercise in esthetics far removed from business life. The successful identity is based on a company's needs, i.e., on its strategy.

The basic reason for a new graphic identity is change—change that has already occurred, or change that management wants to happen. Whenever change occurs or is desired, two basic questions arise: What is the nature of that change? and, What issues arise from or are affected by that change? Determining the issues involved directs the development of the graphic identity.

Some common changes that may signal the need for a new corporate identity include:

• Mergers and acquisitions of companies with conflicting identities and/or differing operations.

• Expansion from within a company into new areas of operation.

• Divestiture of operating units, with a resulting change in the nature of business.

• A strategic alliance with another entity, e.g., a joint venture.

• A change of management or management policy.

• A corporate restructure or reorganization that alters business and communications strategies.

• Problems or changes in one or more markets, e.g., increased competition or the deregulation of an industry.

• An existing identity that is confused or outdated.

• Products that are better known than the corporate signature.

• Subsidiaries within a well-known conglomerate that need more visibility to compete successfully.

• Problems with employee morale.

• A drop in profits or earnings.

• Recruitment problems.

• Problems among divisions, or between divisions and the corporation.

This list shouldn't be read as the last word. Nor do these situations often arise individually. Most large identity projects will include elements of two or more of these conditions, and small businesses will exhibit versions reflecting their own scale and complexity.

It is good to remember that there are prob-

Sometimes an old and venerable mark is adapted for special application within the company. Makers of currency papers and fine stationery since the beginning of the nineteenth century, Crane & Company adopted the figure of a crane as a symbol in 1919 (top). Later, the bird was simplified and incorporated into a watermark to identify one of Crane's all-cotton business papers (center). In 1989 Chermayeff & Geismar Inc. streamlined the design once again for special use by the company's business papers division (bottom).

Citibank. Executed in the early 1970s, First National City Bank's identity change to "Citibank" was a precursor to today's strategic name changes. At the time, 850 American banks had the words "First National" in their names, and FNCB itself operated under more than twenty legal names in the United States alone. Developed by Anspach Grossman Portugal, the new name took the bank back to its roots—it had been founded as City Bank in 1812—and created a component, "Citi-," that could be developed separately. The bank's traditional symbol was modernized and joined to a sleek, ligatured logotype.

lems that a new corporate identity can't solve, and the identity designer must be able to make this distinction. If a company is basically unsound, even the glue of the strongest corporate identity program won't be able to hold it together. Moreover, developing a new identity is a shake-up process in itself. A weak company will not be able to withstand the process, unless management has a strong commitment to using identity as a tool to turn the company around.

A change in corporate identity alone can't alter business strategy, but it can signal that changes in strategy have been made. Corporate identity can't make a bad product good or patch up a badly managed company, either. Clients need to know that, and sometimes it's up to the designer to tell them. Fortunately, since you will likely be well into an identity project before such problems become apparent, you already should have established a healthy relationship with your client. Furthermore, if you've done the homework needed to discover such a condition, you should be able to back up any such observations with hard facts. (See Chapter Two, "Starting the Corporate Identity Process," for more on client relationships and research and analysis.)

Landing a Corporate Identity Job
Identity projects are very sought after because they can offer good fees and enduring relationships for the graphic designer. But how does a designer break into the field? How do you go about finding an identity job?

Because of its association with "art" and "design," graphic identity sometimes is seen as superficial or cosmetic. Despite this perception, identity consultants are increasingly asked to help companies sort out various management problems having to do with identity (who the company is) and image (how the company is perceived). It would be unprofessional, and even unethical, for a designer to try to sell an identity program as if it were a trendy decoration. Corporate identity shouldn't be sold as if it's simply a new letterhead. Nor can it be approached like a one-time promotional campaign.

Unfortunately, some clients may ask you to dash off an identity, and they might even know exactly how it should look. In such cases, explain to your client that graphic identity needs to be expressed in its larger context of marketing and management strategies, and that an identifier should be carefully developed. If your client turns a deaf ear, you have a few options. You can gracefully refuse the job, whose success may be doomed from the start anyway. You can produce the logomark your client has in mind and do your best to make it work. Or you can go through the research and analysis process anyway, design your client's version of a new identity, and then develop another logomark that more dynamically addresses the underlying identity issues (as Midnight Oil did for Souper Salad, pages 104-109). Your personal equation of time, money and initiative will help you choose.

Still, most identity programs get started because the client perceives that the company is in trouble. Sometimes, management only asks for the design of "a bug and a logo." Other times, the client suspects a more serious problem and may, in fact, have a good idea as to what that problem is. It is in these instances that clients ask a designer for help.

This request for assistance may come directly to a designer who has an established relationship with the client, or it may go to a designer referred by a business colleague or a vendor. A client may leaf through design annuals or trade magazines looking for likely consultants. But these are ways in which designers are likely to receive any assignment.

There are instances where you can take the initiative—when you see a client's need for a new graphic identity. This might happen when you become aware of a lack of visual focus in a client's many communications efforts. (Visual chaos often signals internal chaos.) Sometimes, an attitude survey done for another purpose—say, target marketing—reveals a weak or confused identity. Or you may observe that, while a client's products remain the same, there has been a shift in emphasis or service that needs to be signaled through

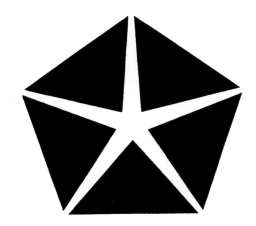

Chrysler. Chrysler Corporation is an interesting example of a company that underwent an identity change, but elected not to change its name. After beating back bankruptcy in the early 1980s, the corporation was restructured to allow expansion into nonautomotive fields. Identity consultants Lippincott & Margulies were called in to examine the "real" and graphic identity issues involved. Although the Chrysler name had come to be associated with the automotive industry through long use, there was nothing inherent in it that would prevent it from being applied to other lines of business. Lippincott recommended that Chrysler keep its name (which, incidentally, was the name of its founder) and also its "pentastar" symbol. The pair then became the cornerstone of a new graphic identity program aimed at repositioning the corporation for expansion and clarifying its relation with its operating units.

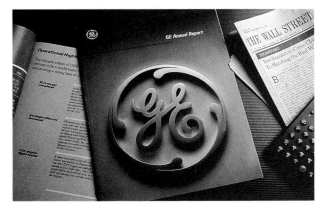

GE. The story of General Electric is a classic case of why a company adopts its initials as its name. General Electric was founded by Thomas Edison in 1878. The original script "GE" appeared sometime in the 1890s, possibly as the center decoration for an electric fan. In 1899, it was adopted as a general trademark and survives to this day, though not without much scrutiny. In an identity review undertaken by Landor Associates in 1986 at the company's request, it was discovered that the full name,

General Electric, made its audience think of "small appliances" and "outdated activities." Since GE had divested itself of its small electronics and held core businesses in technology, manufacturing and financial services, the full name was neither positive nor accurate. Landor recommended adopting the universally recognized "GE" as the corporate name and gently restyled the old script monogram to enhance its perception.

identity. In short, if you are aware of what graphic identity is, how it operates, and its strategic importance to a company, you should be able to recognize when it's missing. Then you'll need to communicate that observation to the client.

But that doesn't necessarily precipitate an identity assignment. Some clients are by nature suspicious of design and still see it as a decoration or a frill. They may feel that graphic identity is an unavoidable business expense like advertising and sales promotion, but that it isn't as important.

Also, people generally don't like change. Changing a company's name or graphic image tears at all kinds of emotional attachments. A client may see such change as too risky. After all, it takes real courage for anyone to become who they really want to be, and letting go of who you are — even if it isn't working — is always a painful process.

Once clients are convinced that a new corporate identity is to the company's advantage, they still may not trust an outsider to do the job, or to solve "management" issues. Respond by using the very reasons a company needs a new identity as your selling points.

The Benefits of a New Identity. Time and again, strategic changes in identity have had a positive impact on key business yardsticks such as sales and stock prices. By pointing out the strengths and weaknesses of a company and its existing identity, and by explaining how a new identity program would address these issues, a designer can sometimes convince a client of genuine need.

Too, most businesses already spend considerable sums on advertising and sales promotion, packaging, and all sorts of communications. If these expenditures are only promoting confusion, how much better — and smarter — to put them all under the unifying banner of an effective graphic identity program! True, there will be an additional expense to implement the identity change, but effective identity saves money in the long run, through likely increases in sales and earnings, and simply because it stops waste.

In a large corporation, if the share price/earnings ratio increases even a few points because of a monetary investment in a new corporate identity, the company quickly recoups the expense. Because identity programs for smaller businesses are proportionately less costly yet still yield tangible results, they, too, can quickly pay for themselves.

Developing a new identity forces a company to seriously assess strategic elements it may be taking for granted: planning; personnel; long-term goals and how to reach them; and how the company is being perceived, compared with how it would like to be perceived. By actively discussing these issues, managers and other employees become more intimately involved in the direction of the company. And, whatever their division or rank, they find themselves working together toward a shared goal.

As the identity process continues, it becomes a rallying point for employees at all levels, catalyzing improved employee relations. At the same time, it enhances recruitment by attracting a better grade of employee.

To those outside the company, a new corporate identity signals internal change. It draws attention to a company, effecting a kind of renaissance before its audiences. Because it clearly explains who, what and where, a new identity attracts more business, new accounts, and larger orders from larger and more important customers.

As public perception of the company improves, so do vendor and supplier relationships, as everyone wants to be associated with a perceived leader. By minimizing mixed messages and clearing up any ambiguities, the new identity builds a new confidence in the public mind. The company finds itself better able to address any problems it might have in its public image. And it's now better positioned to make those strategic moves—into new markets, for example, or into additional product lines.

Be Prepared. Having convinced the client of the need for a new corporate identity, you may still need to sell yourself. One way to do this is by exuding confidence in your authority as a designer while addressing the client's need for a new graphic identity. But clients need to see more

than confidence.

For example, a client who hesitates to hire an outside identity consultant needs to be reassured that an outsider just may be the best person for the job. First, corporate designers and communicators aren't always well versed in issues of corporate identity. A company designer will be steeped in the corporate culture, but this isn't always an asset when trying to gain perspective on identity problems. Outsiders are often better qualified to assess a company's communications problems simply because they bring a certain objectivity to the task. There is nothing for the outsider to guard or defend, no ego invested (unless, of course, she was the designer of the original identity), no emotional attachment to tradition.

Independent designers can more easily place themselves in the shoes of the company's average customer. They can bring external, "real-world" values to bear on identity issues and make recommendations unbiased by familiarity. And they can work through the identity process without having to play political games, speaking their minds to top decision makers without fear of repercussion.

In addition, clients have justifiable concerns about handing their company's strategic image—and future—over to just anyone. They want to know that the designer they hire has the skill and experience to both develop an effective identity and see it through implementation. They need to be assured that whoever they hire understands the company, its strategies, and the issues that need to be addressed. They need a designer who gets along well with whatever personalities will be involved in the identity process, whether a lone entrepreneurial decision maker or a corporate identity committee. And, of course, the client has to like the designer's work.

The Best Designer for the Job
You can take some steps to facilitate getting an identity job. Of course, you should have a professional portfolio on hand to leave with prospective clients. If you have experience in corporate identity, you might want to prepare a dedicated portfolio of your work in this area. This could be the

Many designers build identity portfolios by doing work for non-profits, such as this piece by Rickabaugh Graphics for Directions for Youth, a nonprofit organization for troubled teens. These will often be low budget or pro bono projects but can be invaluable in terms of experience and exposure.

typical zippered binder with printed samples of identity applications, or it could be a more elaborate affair. Some designers focus on graphic marks and present primarily black-and-white photo prints of symbols and logotypes. Others show printed samples of complete programs with photographs of three-dimensional applications. One design firm has an "identity box"—a handsomely covered, hard-sided case with stacks of foam-core-mounted samples inside. The samples can be edited to target the prospect.

A designer trying to break into the field can get invaluable real-world experience by doing nonprofit and pro bono identity work. Though such organizations usually work with low budgets, they often compensate by offering designers the chance to do truly innovative work.

Or you can create projects for imaginary companies by taking the role of both client and designer. Your samples should include the items typically shown to the client at the first design presentation: the logomark and its application to stationery, printed communications, advertising, signage and vehicles. Despite the fictitious nature of the project, you should handle it like a real project and go through all the steps required to create an effective graphic identity.

While ordinarily designers should not submit identity (or any other) designs on speculation, there are instances when taking initiative pays. If, for example, you're hired to do a packaging job and it becomes apparent that identity issues are involved, a comp or two, showing the client the possibilities to be realized with a new identity, could result in an assignment of much larger scope. Sayles Graphic Design's identity program for Schaffer's Bridal & Formal Wear came about in just this way.

Showing the client sample identity solutions, even if hypothetical, is an important part of winning client confidence. If clients are going to entrust the future of their company to a designer, spend tens or even hundreds of thousands of dollars, and experience a good deal of pain and internal upset because of it, they have to know that that trust is well placed.

Energy Department Store

A retail store featuring energy conserving hard goods and natural fiber clothing and accessories.

The symbol integrates the federal government's energy conservation lower-case "e" with the three natural energy sources—sun, wind, and water.

While a portfolio of completed identity projects clearly shows your skill at and experience with identity design, you can build an effective portfolio in other ways. You can show logomarks with a brief explanation about the client and the reasoning behind the design. The example here is from Katz Wheeler's identity box—an attractive box containing carefully displayed samples of their logomark and identity work. You can also show samples of letterhead designs.

When the owner of Schaffer's Bridal & Formal Wear asked John Sayles to design new hangtags for garments being delivered to customers, Sayles quickly realized that the shop really needed a new complete identity program. A weekend's hard work produced comps of the hangtags and several other pieces that landed Sayles a job designing a complete package for the bridal shop, including stationery, hangtags, boxes, bags, and even clothing for the employees (see page 55 for more on these items).

Starting the Corporate Identity Process

Graphic identity must be grounded in who the client is: the nature of the company's business, its traditions and culture, its products, services and markets. The process of developing a visual identity for any business can be divided into four major areas of work and expertise:

1. Research and analysis—in which the designer learns all about the client.

2. Design development—in which the designer develops a graphic identity based on the findings of research and analysis.

3. Design application—in which the designer tackles the real work of bringing all of the client's visual communications into the identity program.

4. Design implementation—in which the solutions, standards and guidelines of design application become a graphic reality.

As a process, these steps build one upon the other. All are essential if an identity program is to be truly complete and effective. This chapter focuses on the first of these stages: initial fact-finding and determining the client's needs.

The Designer-Client Relationship

A designer learns about a client in many ways and, in learning, lays the foundation for a strong designer-client relationship. This relationship, in turn, will help build a strong identity program.

Because most corporate identity issues are also management issues, it is imperative that corporate identity designers also see themselves as management consultants. To effectively navigate the identity process, they need to get inside the corporate head and become an invisible member of the corporate management team. They have to operate from a position that is fully informed about the client they serve.

Working on a large corporate identity project can be a rewarding experience, especially if management has a single vision and is fully committed to the identity process. Corporate officers are used to delegating responsibility and so are likely to let you do your job without a lot of interference. Large companies also tend to be more literate in looking at and talking about graphic design. And large projects offer the opportunity to develop an identity for a broader range of applications, with greater visibility and commensurately higher fees.

On the other hand, policies in large companies are often made by committee, and senior management is often composed of major shareholders. Unless the chief executive officer has a strong personality with the full cooperation of his officers, a corporation will seldom have one driving force. Instead, layers and layers of management will yield the stereotypical corporation, grown cold and stodgy and less willing to take risks.

Dealing with a small business client can be quite a different experience. For one thing, small businesses—even the more complicated ones—are often run by one strong personality. This makes them easier to deal with, simply because they are more intuitive. In addition, they are usually more responsive than a large corporation that operates through levels of bureaucracy.

Here, too, designers often enjoy direct access to the person at the top—there's no wading through the committee process, and there's much less company politicking to deal with. The small business person is often an entrepreneur used to acting alone and making quick decisions, and this alone can relieve you of a lot of headaches. There is a certain amount of gratification in such personal contact and the appreciation that can ensue. Moreover, if you can tap into and gain the confidence of a small business's top person, it will be easier to develop a visual identity that is truly individual and unique.

However, some small business owners are relatively unsophisticated about graphic design. In such cases, you will also have to be an educator. By explaining the benefits of a clear graphic identity, by revealing how it supports larger business strategies, and by making clear what good design can and can't do, you can establish yourself as an expert in visual communications and pave the way for mutual trust.

If you seek to design graphic identity for colleagues and friends, take special care never to deviate from professional form. You must manage work for such a client as professionally and as thoroughly as you would for any other. In such instances, good business practices—prompt meetings, follow-up memoranda, strict adherence to deadlines—are especially important for responsible identity management, or the relationship may become too casual.

When your client is also your vendor or supplier—a photographer, type house or printer with whom you also work—you face the possibility of making too many assumptions. An identity designer needs to know all the facets of a client's business, and your being a customer of that vendor or supplier doesn't necessarily mean you know about other aspects of their business.

The First Meeting. Prepare for the first meeting with a new corporate identity client by asking for background materials beforehand. These might include samples of existing identity materials, capabilities brochures, product bulletins, annual reports—any printed materials aimed at the company's public. Larger companies can easily supply these; smaller ones might require research.

Reading this material enables you to go into the meeting informed and thus able to ask intelligent questions. And it will also inspire trust and confidence from the very first meeting, perhaps even helping you to land the job.

Once you have the commission, meet with the client to discuss general expectations. At this point, the client will explain in greater detail why the company's identity needs to be examined. He should be very clear as to what he expects the new identity to accomplish, and, again, you may have to explain the benefits and limitations of a good visual identity.

At this meeting, explain the development and design processes and the routine for assessing fees and submitting bills. (For more on this, see "Estimating Costs" on pages 30-33.) If a client has not had much experience with the design process, it's also a good idea to bring along sketches, comps and finishes from other jobs. This will give him tangible examples of what you'll produce for the fee, and will also help him interpret the roughs and comps that you'll present later.

This meeting is also the time for both parties to define their roles in the identity process and to set up a structure for identity management. If the company is somewhat large (a big corporation or a smaller business with several divisions or operating units), the client will probably form a committee to oversee the day-to-day business of identity development. You will then report your progress to this committee.

The working committee should represent various corporate interests and be drawn from all areas of management and operations. Because its members are sensitive to the many political issues within the company, it can become an invaluable sounding board for an identity designer.

Regardless of size, client companies don't always have a natural liaison to head up this committee or to deal with the daily issues of identity design. Therefore, try to find the best possible person within the client company to serve as identity liaison. This person should be in a position of authority, with direct access to top management. In a large corporation, the liaison might be a com-

munications officer or the vice-president in charge of corporate affairs; in a smaller company, it could be an operations manager or an executive assistant. The CEO or business owner should be present at the first meeting to make his needs known, and then be on hand for hard decision making.

Many designers with experience in corporate identity feel it is not advisable for CEOs (or those in ultimate authority) to personally manage identity development: They simply aren't used to thinking of their companies' problems in terms of identity issues or as being related to identity. In very small businesses or in sole proprietorships, however, you may not have any choice—the owner will be the identity liaison.

The CEO or business owner *is* the best person to make the final decisions about an identity program, because his authority will carry great weight in enforcing implementation. To that end, request that he issue a company-wide announcement that a graphic identity review is underway. This letter should also state the reasons the project has been undertaken and who is doing it. It should also emphasize the importance of the project to the future of the company and encourage everyone to cooperate in any requests for materials or confidential interviews.

Finally, from the first meeting, you must listen well. Indeed, the quality of your listening may well be the determining factor in developing effective identity. Some designers tape-record all of their meetings and confidential interviews with managers and employees; others prefer to jot down the most salient points. Use whatever means best fit your style, but *listen and remember*. When it comes to selling the final design, a playback of the client's stated needs and objectives, joined to a solution that meets those points, can be a persuasive tool.

Project Management. Whether you work alone or with others, you must create a system for managing the identity process within your firm. Duties might include client service, project direction (combining creative thinking, design strategizing and administration), and design and production (for which the practitioner will need a fertile imagination, design and typographic skills, knowledge of papers and printing, and the ability to produce under pressure). In large design shops, these duties may be divided among several employees, from account supervisors and creative directors to individual designers and production people. In this case, the senior employees will meet with the client committee and relay information to the design team. Smaller design studios will have to accomplish the same goals with fewer people—maybe even a single individual.

The client's working committee can share some of the burden of identity development; don't be afraid to make use of the committee's skills. Members can conduct interviews within areas of their expertise and discuss identity problems among themselves. They can put their findings into a formal report and make their own recommendations.

Involving clients from the start helps them make the identity project their own. If clients invest considerable time and energy in the investigative and development phases, they will be more highly motivated to implement the results.

At the same time, it is up to you to manage client involvement as a positive force. Any client representatives involved should have a thorough understanding of the identity process—what it is and how it works to develop a graphic identity system. The designer may have to coach the committee on this to some extent.

At regular intervals during the identity process, report your progress to the client. This can be done casually through telephone calls to, for example, settle minor questions or report piecemeal progress; or more formally at meetings with the identity liaison or whole committee. You also will need to keep in touch with any individual committee members responsible for specific tasks.

However, be wary of showing the client developmental materials such as sources and sketches. While some designers use them to document their thinking during presentation of the final design, many feel that showing early, rejected ideas

only courts catastrophe. Unless the client is truly visually literate and has complete faith in the designer's discretion, he could latch onto an inappropriate, discarded form, thus deflecting the identity process from its course. Pursuing what you know to be blind alleys is both costly and time-consuming. But perhaps worst of all, you may be forced into using the rejected idea. If you want to let the client exercise the power of choice, offer one or two alternative solutions when presenting the final design.

Gathering Information

In addition to gathering insights from client meetings, you should collect as much information about the client company as possible and interpret and analyze it thoroughly. The object is to examine the nature and structure of the company and how it is perceived from both inside and out. This evaluation will yield a clearer definition of the client's identity issues and help establish goals for identity development. It is imperative that this phase be thorough, for a missed step or overlooked application here could throw off a later solution.

Specifically, you will want to be alert for information about:

1. The historical development of the company.

2. Corporate philosophy: how the company treats its employees; its attitudes toward shareholders and customers; its business practices; its sense of responsibility toward the communities in which it operates.

3. Its organization and legal structure (this will influence naming and development of visual hierarchies).

4. Marketing data: the company's position in the marketplace, past and present marketing strategies, how it stacks up against the competition.

5. How employees, customers, suppliers and the financial community feel about the company and its products/services.

Printed Materials. One of your first requests of the client should be access to all communica-

Fifteen Questions to Ask a Corporate Identity Client

As one designer puts it, "When the client is asked the right questions, the answers practically determine the identity." These fifteen questions are typical of the kinds designers ask clients in order to define corporate identity issues.

1. Why have you called a designer to do a new graphic identity? What changes in the company have signaled this need? What are the issues on the minds of management?

2. What are the simple basics about the company: its parts or divisions, products, services, people and markets?

3. What is the company's history? How has its business changed since it was started? Since five or ten years ago? What changes do you anticipate for the future?

4. How does the company do business? How does it sell its products/services?

5. What is management's vision of the company? Who do they think the company behind the basics is?

6. What is the management style — centralized or decentralized, linked divisions or autonomous subsidiaries? How do different locations of a small business relate to headquarters?

7. Who are your important publics — employees, customers, potential customers, government, community, investors, analysts? How does the company interface with them?

8. What does the company do well? Not do well?

9. Is the company or its products/services difficult to understand? Why? What would management rather be understood?

10. How do you think the company is perceived by its audiences? What evidence supports your impressions?

11. How accurate are audience perceptions? Where and how are they inaccurate? How does management want the company to be seen? (These questions reveal exact issues of identity any solution must address.)

12. How does the company's existing graphic identity support management's vision? Is that identity distinctive from competitors'?

13. Do all visual aspects of the company look like they come from the same company? Do existing graphics relate to one another?

14. Does the company have specific communications objectives? What are they? How well has the current identity system been meeting them?

15. How does the company currently purchase graphic and communications design? Are there in-house designers or outside studios and agencies? What are their jobs, and how will they be utilized in developing a new identity?

These questions are designed to elicit revealing responses from management, but they could also be used, with a few changes, to interview key outsiders — major customers, for example. The view from the outside will likely be a little different, and perhaps very instructive. Those inside a company may be too involved in daily business to see their problems clearly.

tions the company has issued in the past several years — advertisements, brochures, annual reports, press releases — whatever the company has used to explain itself to one or more audiences. If the company is an old and venerable one, archival materials will also be of interest — and may even contain an appropriate solution. (Refer to the Sleeman Brewing and Malting Company Case

Study, shown on pages 100-103.)

Get newsclips, too, as well as any round-up stories about the industry that may have appeared in trade journals or the financial press. If the client has not collected such information for its own files, you'll have to research it, either at the library or directly from the publishers. These stories will reveal problems faced by the client and its competition industrywide.

Read reports from any research or marketing studies the client has executed. (If it's necessary—and the budget allows—the designer can commission research studies specific to corporate identity issues.) However, most small businesses don't need expensive marketing studies and design testing. Their owners usually know their business, markets, customers, and who they want the company to be.

Interviews. Any company will have strategies to project its image while growing its business and increasing profits. The interviews conducted during the initial phase of the identity process should reveal those strategies and their influence on the company's perceived identity. In doing so, they will also suggest how both strategy and identity need to be adjusted so that the company can more easily achieve its business goals.

In conducting the interviews, look beyond what is seen and heard and consider deeper meanings. Take information across boundaries, and correlate and integrate it. A shabby lobby area says something about how the company sees itself, as well as reflecting how it welcomes visitors. During interviews with client executives, keep in mind the basic ways in which businesses are organized. (Refer back to pages 6-8.) This will alert you to any discrepancies between the way the company is actually managed and the way it looks like it's managed.

It's worth repeating that you should write down the points management says need to be addressed, so they can be used later to justify an identity solution. Clients need to know what their strategic wishes actually mean in terms of graphic identity.

When interviewing people under the top brass, don't be afraid to get personal. Interviewing should be as informal as possible, with one to two hours allowed for each conversation. Once the interviewee is at ease, more pointed questions can be introduced, such as, "What's it like working for this company?" Other personal questions might be: "How do you fit in? How do your superiors treat you?" When confidentiality is guaranteed and employees can speak without fear of repercussion, truth will out.

Finally, if the company has several far-flung locations and the budget doesn't permit travel to all of them for interviews, you can use a questionnaire and follow up with phone calls. However, a questionnaire should be only a last resort. Many recipients will ignore them or be too busy to fill them out. And those who do respond may not be willing to put their real feelings in writing.

The Visual Audit. Although you will have done an initial visual audit to get a general impression of the company and its communications, once the interview process is complete, you will want to review all the company's communications again. A comprehensive review should include not only printed materials but also any TV or radio advertising, billboards and signage. Check out the physical facilities beyond signage: vehicles and their state of repair, the interior and exterior of retail outlets or restaurants, the design of any products and their packaging. Photograph as many facilities as possible to see where corporate identity can be more effectively applied and to help the client visualize the true nature of the problem. In this way, you'll get a complete picture of how the company presents itself to its different audiences, and of how these presentations relate to one another.

At the same time, collect as many examples as possible of what the client's competitors are doing. This is especially important if the client wants to expand markets, product lines or types of business. The point is to create a visual identity that is appropriate and distinctive to both the company's personality and its market conditions.

A communications audit will often reveal a lack of coherent corporate identity. If the com-

Fourteen Questions to Ask Yourself When Doing a Visual Audit

Here are some things to look for when conducting a design/communications audit:

1. How is the company's name being used? What does that say about the organization?

2. What types of materials are used, and how? Is there any duplication? How could that be eliminated?

3. How do these materials relate to one another visually, verbally — and in light of the company's stated goals?

4. Is there consistency in style? Do materials have a specific personality, or could they be anybody's?

5. How do these materials compare with what the competition is doing? What does the client need to compete successfully against current and future competitors?

6. Is there an apparent design policy? Are related products or services visually connected? Should they be?

7. How is type being handled — to clarify or confuse? With or without purpose?

8. Are communications being issued by each unit/location, or by the company as a whole? How effective is this?

9. How do communications from the main office compare with those issued at other offices/facilities?

10. Do different parts of the company come across as being parts of the whole? Should they?

11. Do communications from any one unit suggest that this area is second class?

12. What is the physical condition of the company's facilities? Are offices and vehicles shabby?

13. Does the condition change depending on who uses the facilities?

14. Are printed materials poorly produced? What kind of impressions do they convey?

---

pany has several strong brands, these may need to be brought under an umbrella identity that still allows their individuality. Or individual operating units of varying renown might benefit from being unified under a single well-known name.

The audit also reveals where and how the company has been spending its design and communications budget. For example, do employee publications pale beside sales promotions? How does the client account for any discrepancies? Sometimes it's not a matter of policy — the client simply may never have considered how communications dollars have been meted out. The identity designer has a real opportunity here not only to bring a range of communications into the new system, but to develop a meaningful and more wide-ranging communications plan.

Similarly, the client may never have seen the range of the company's communications all together before and so has been completely oblivious to its coherency — or lack of it. Sometimes such a display is the most persuasive evidence you can offer for the need for a graphic identity and communications overhaul.

At this point, you might also talk with the people who have been responsible for previous communications to find out how they have understood the company's goals as expressed in its communications policies. How have these goals been carried out? What has been the relationship between communications and marketing? What kind of supervision have the people had, or not had?

In the research phases of the identity process for National Distillers and Chemical Corporation, Landor Associates reviewed the company's identity practices and printed communications. The identity consultants found that, since the parent company and each of its three subsidiaries had such diverse identities (top), there was no cross-recognition and no suggestion that all four were part of the same organization. Moreover, a study of printed communications from all four units (bottom) revealed that even these individual identities were not being used with consistency — creating only further confusion. Since each business was a leader in its own market, the client was missing benefits that might accrue from linking their identities.

Analysis

After you compare the existing corporate identity and communications program with the corporate and strategic goals gathered from interviews, the client's problems should be obvious. They will appear wherever there is any discrepancy between stated goals ("This is who we are or want to be and how we want to look") and the perceived reality ("This is how we look"). The objectives for design development are built around what it will take to bring the reality in line with the stated goals. They will also explain how changes in the identity system will accomplish or support this task.

In asking how well the company's current identity does its job, you'll begin to identify what's missing — what the identity needs to maximize its effectiveness. This might be a single identifying element, such as a mark or logotype, that will link all parts of a company; a clear naming system; a more unified approach to communications; or all of these. But an identity overhaul can't solve all the problems a company faces.

Sometimes a thorough analysis of a company's culture and communications turns up some unpleasant surprises. You may discover serious discrepancies between the way a company imagines itself to be and the way the public actually perceives it. Client interviews may reveal a disgruntled management or departments that thwart one another's efforts. As a designer charged with certain management responsibilities, it is your duty to bring these discoveries to your client's attention; they are areas to be addressed, both by the new identity and by corporate management.

Informing clients of their shortcomings needn't be a traumatic experience. Although some entrepreneur's egos may be particularly identified with their companies, most managers will still want to hear about any suspected areas of mismanagement. After all, their businesses — and their personal livelihoods — may depend on it.

The key is to approach the subject as an opportunity for positive and constructive change. Tell the client, as gracefully and as tactfully as possible, just what difficulties have been discovered and where the sources seem to lie. Offer ways for management to address these problems: for example, strengthening internal reporting procedures, reformulating products, or developing more dynamic marketing strategies. And, of course, show how the new identity will support any restructuring efforts, and incorporate those points into the identity criteria.

Another part of analysis deals with determining the range or extent of a proposed identity overhaul. For a large corporation, this could mean making sense of several divisions or operating units and a lot of corporate and divisional communications pieces. For the smaller client, it may mean bringing coherence to a few products and services and several communications pieces. It may also mean suggesting better ways of doing things—replacing sheaves of paperwork with a few standardized, well-thought-out forms, for example. A materials and budget analysis might reveal that the client could more economically produce stationery and forms at one central location rather than jobbing out piecemeal orders through individual divisions or locations. All of this falls within the range of opportunity for an identity consultant.

Stylistic identity changes are the general rule, and they can range from radical to evolutionary. An identity that is outmoded, outdated, inappropriate or no longer workable may have to be scrapped entirely. The designer will then use the objectives established through research and analysis to devise a new and more appropriate identity.

Occasionally a new name is called for, due to a merger or the name no longer matching what the company does. But name changes are expensive, involve a lot of legal work, and create massive emotional difficulties. Generally, they aren't worth it unless there is no other way around a company's problems.

Evolutionary change—a sort of fine-tuning of an existing identity—is called for when there have been no radical changes in the client's business and when the company's visual style is already powerful and appropriate. It could be that

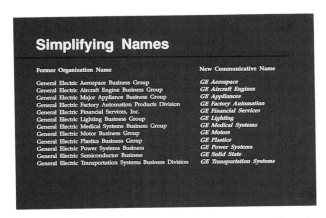

Simplifying Names

Former Organization Name	New Communicative Name
General Electric Aerospace Business Group	GE Aerospace
General Electric Aircraft Engine Business Group	GE Aircraft Engines
General Electric Major Appliance Business Group	GE Appliances
General Electric Factory Automation Products Division	GE Factory Automation
General Electric Financial Services, Inc.	GE Financial Services
General Electric Lighting Business Group	GE Lighting
General Electric Medical Systems Business Group	GE Medical Systems
General Electric Motor Business Group	GE Motors
General Electric Plastics Business Group	GE Plastics
General Electric Power Systems Business	GE Power Systems
General Electric Semiconductor Business	GE Solid State
General Electric Transportation Systems Business Division	GE Transportation Systems

General Electric's name change to its already-familiar initials was an evolutionary one, but Landor Associates' application of the name to operating groups was considerably different. The new naming system sought to simplify internal organizational names and executive titles, as well as emphasize the company's diversity. The common denominator in each case is the corporate "GE," plus a simple but appropriate generic identifier.

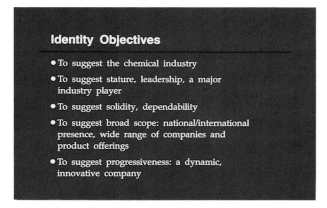

Identity Objectives

- To suggest the chemical industry
- To suggest stature, leadership, a major industry player
- To suggest solidity, dependability
- To suggest broad scope: national/international presence, wide range of companies and product offerings
- To suggest progressiveness: a dynamic, innovative company

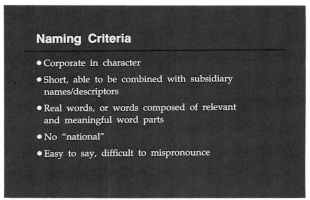

Naming Criteria

- Corporate in character
- Short, able to be combined with subsidiary names/descriptors
- Real words, or words composed of relevant and meaningful word parts
- No "national"
- Easy to say, difficult to mispronounce

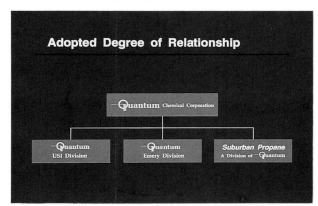

Adopted Degree of Relationship

Quantum Chemical Corporation

| Quantum USI Division | Quantum Emery Division | Suburban Propane A Division of Quantum |

The former National Distillers and Chemical Corporation had been composed of three divisions—USI Chemicals, Emery Chemicals and Suburban Propane—each operating under its own name. From their visual audit and interviews with executives, Landor Associates developed these identity and naming objectives (top, center), which were put on 35mm slides and presented to the client. The name and design development phases resulted in a name change and linked identities (bottom). While its sister companies adopted the new name of the parent company, Quantum, the Suburban Propane name was too well known to be used as a divisional name. It therefore remained that division's primary identifier, and the corporate signature became an endorsement.

a slight shift of emphasis or a "clean-up" of the logotype is all that is needed. In such cases, redesigning the primary visual identifier may be minimal, but its reapplication may be radically different. (See Chrysler Corporation and GE, pages 15-16, for two companies who fine-tuned their existing identity.)

At the end of the analysis, you'll prepare a written statement of the results of your information gathering. This, along with a cost estimate, forms the basis for establishing the parameters of the new identity program. It will take the form of a list of recommended objectives, based on needs cited in client interviews and your own analysis of the client's existing identity/communications system. In general, these criteria describe what the ideal identity for that company should achieve—for instance, making the company look "dynamic," "progressive," etc.; continuing the traditions of the past or breaking with them; providing the base for clear marketing communications; clarifying areas of confusion; showing economic feasibility; being applicable to a range of communications. The important thing is that the criteria—however many or few—grapple with fundamental identity issues.

Estimating Costs

Once you have formalized the design objectives, write up cost estimates for your client presentation. The estimate should contain information concerning the types, sizes and number of pieces to be included; coordination of implementation phases; typography, printing, binding and delivery charges; any other production costs; and fees for identity research, design development and implementation. Reimbursable expenses such as telephone and travel should also be itemized. Once approved by the client, the written cost estimate becomes the basis for a project contract. (See the sample form on page 32.)

The cost of a company's identity overhaul will depend on many factors. One of these is its size. Generally the bigger the company, the more complex it is and the more work involved in researching, designing and implementing an identity program. A good place to start a cost estimate is with the client's budget. While the first question some clients ask is, "How much is this going to cost?" most clients know roughly how much they have to spend on any given design project. It's your responsibility to use that money wisely.

Most identity designers like to establish a budget at the outset of the project. Identity design fees can range from a few hundred dollars for a simple nonprofit, logomark-and-letterhead identity (when they're not done pro bono), to a few million dollars to design and implement an identity for a major corporation with hundreds of applications. The Graphic Artists Guild (30 E. 20th Street, New York, NY 10012) publishes current pricing guidelines and sample contracts; its *Handbook of Pricing & Ethical Guidelines* (available from North Light Books) is a good reference. Hourly rates for design alone can run upward from forty dollars to several hundred, depending on the client and the size and reputation of the design firm. Design fees run lower in some areas due to local factors.

Once the client has suggested a ball-park figure, you can assess whether the amount is realistic. As you complete the interviewing and research, the amount of work necessary to reach the company's goals should be clear. Will there be many sets of stationery (divisional, sales, other) involved? Is there a need for publications guidelines? Are there vehicles? Is there architectural signage? Each additional facet of identity will take time to bring into the new identity system, and you'll have to estimate how much time will be needed and how much it will cost. (Chapter Four provides a more complete list of application possibilities.)

Suppliers are probably the most important source for putting together estimated or probable costs. As you begin to establish the parameters of the identity project, contact suppliers for pricing assistance. A paper sales rep, for example, can show what types of business papers are available, in what quantities, within a given price range; a printing rep can answer questions about the cost of adding a second color to corporate stationery,

for example, or where to obtain printed napkins and other paper goods for a fast-food client. Architectural sign companies can supply fabrication and cost data about various materials, and automotive painters about applying identity to vehicles. In short, you'll have to research every aspect of application for materials and cost, in order to draw up a budget and establish the parameters for the job.

If a company's purchasing department will place the print orders for the actual pieces, consult them about their preferred suppliers for routine restocking of business materials. Ask them which types of identity-related materials they regularly order, and find out the quantities and frequency of those orders. This information can be used in costing-out program applications. Too often purchasing agents have been drilled to simply go for the cheapest price. You (and the identity manager, if there is one) can also use this opportunity to impress upon purchasing personnel the importance of meeting your design specifications: No corners can be cut if they compromise quality.

Make current suppliers aware of their client's quality needs, and lead them along to meet higher standards, if necessary. Many suppliers welcome the opportunity to upgrade their skills, as it helps them attract a better grade of client themselves.

If a client thinks your fees are too high, your willingness to negotiate could save the situation. Look for areas of responsibility that the client can assume. For example, if there is historical material to be researched, let the client do the rough cut. This saves the client a few hours in fees and saves you the tedious task of searching through boxes of old files. Your time can be used more effectively in making design decisions.

Consider whether all of the implementation will be done by your firm, or by the client and/or its advertising agency. This is an especially important consideration in designing for small businesses, many of which simply cannot afford to hire a professional designer for an ongoing implementation program. In such cases, you'll have to provide the client with application guidelines and

Bennett Peji Design

——

Date: 00/00/00
Job Number: 00000
Completion Date: 00/00/00

□ **Contract**
□ **Estimate**

1110
Torrey
Pines Rd
Suite B
La Jolla
California
92037
619
456-
8071

A G R E E M E N T

CLIENT:
Client Contact/Company

PROJECT TITLE
Title

PROJECT BEGINS UPON RECEIPT OF 50% DEPOSIT.
This bid is based on the presentation of a comprehensive mock-up, rough layouts, research, concept and design plus client consultation throughout the project.. All production costs to camera-ready art including typesetting and stats are included. Printing costs are not yet included, however, all print coordination and supervision is included.

Cost Estimate: $0000 +/- 10%

Deposit of 50% to begin project : $0000

FEES:
Consultation:
Design/Layout:
Art Direction:
Administration:
Production:
Print Supervision:
Conference:

OTHER EXPENSES:
Copywriting:
Illustration:
Typesetting:
Photography:
Linos/Stats:
Printing:
Separations:
Fabrication:
Installation:
Delivery:
Telephone/Fax:
Shipping/Handling:
Travel:

Subtotal:
Tax:

TOTAL:

Agreed by and Dated:

* These expenses are contingent upon costs incurred during completion of project.

Samples to be provided for design firm promotions_____.

All rights are reserved for the contractor, Bennett Peji Design, to photograph any portion of this project and to use said photographs or other forms of reproduction as means of self-promotion and publicity for said contractor. Anything not covered in this contract will be billed to client as an additional expense. In the event of cancellation of this assignment, a cancellation fee for work completed, based on the contract price and expenses already incurred, shall be paid by the client.

This form does double duty for designer Bennett Peji, serving as either a contract or a cost-estimate form. Client expenses are clearly spelled out, and space for the client signature is provided.

trust him to use them properly. Or you can make arrangements to monitor, on a consulting basis, any application he does. This will cost him some money, but not as much as for full implementation.

The budget will also be affected by whether a new program will be implemented overnight or on an attrition basis; the more materials involved, the greater the potential savings from attrition. For example, you could suggest waiting to print forms and stationery with the new identity until supplies of the old are exhausted. As new business papers would have to be printed anyway, the only real additional cost to the client here is design time. Otherwise, large quantities of business papers may have to be trashed.

At the same time, it's important that an identity program not be designed and implemented solely from the viewpoint of the bottom line. Some clients may need to dispel a negative image with the "splash" of an all-encompassing, one-time identity launch. And since the standardizing of stationery, forms and other business communications will save the client money in the long run—and the new identity can be expected to generate additional income—there is no point in skimping on its application.

Companies whose identity/image problems include buildings, vehicles, and other more or less permanent fixtures face perhaps the largest challenge to upgrade. Here, costs can be kept down by sprucing up rather than by replacing big-ticket items. Paint a truck instead of replacing it. Fully redecorate only the more public spaces of the client's plant. (But do freshen up employee areas, or there may be a loss of morale.)

Another key to cost management is not to be trapped into conventional thinking. For instance, designers and clients both generally assume the need for a complete stationery system. But are all those pieces really necessary? How many letters does a small business person such as a dry cleaner or hairdresser write? Perhaps all that's needed are business cards, discount coupons, and bill-payer envelopes. It doesn't pay to waste a client's money on applications they'll never use.

Look for alternative production solutions that will lower client costs—designing pieces that can be ganged on press, perhaps, or negotiating with suppliers for better deals. A printing rep will be glad to discuss how to use paper sizes more economically, can advise on alternate production methods, and will even entertain creative pricing if it means a bigger printing job now, or more jobs down the road.

The Client Presentation

Before you begin any design exploration, take the client through the research process and explain the rationale upon which the new identity will be undertaken. Meet with key client representatives, the client working committee (if there is one), or, in a large corporation, the board of directors. Those present will then take the recommendations back to other interested employees.

For best results, the presentation meeting should include visuals highlighting the discoveries made during the interviewing and information-gathering process. Some designers put telling examples of the client's existing graphic identity onto boards and pass them around. Others make a slide presentation of roughly the same material. Make available a typewritten or printed copy of the findings and resulting recommendations for clients to take with them and discuss with their peers.

This comprehensive presentation serves several purposes. First, it focuses everyone's thinking toward real identity issues, so that the next phase, design development, is less likely to become a beauty contest. Moreover, by bringing out the substantive issues involved, it's easier to set priorities and clearly see the extent of the project.

Your recommendations here provide clear criteria and a basis of agreement between you and your client. These points remain as touchstones throughout development, design and implementation phases, allowing objective judgments to be made. Having the client agree to these criteria before you begin design development can help avoid costly misunderstandings later on.

These criteria also help you "sell" the need

What to Take to the Client Presentation

To give credence to your recommendations, you need to lead your clients through the highlights of the interview and research process. Bring along visual aids (slides or printed materials mounted on boards, as well as handouts) that show:

• A description of the company—its past and present, its products or services, and its managing structure.

• Its markets and the competition in those markets.

• The client's current graphic identity in various applications, including where it works and where it doesn't.

• A mass of incoherent communications.

(See "The Visual Audit," pages 26-27.)

• Identities of competing businesses.

• A summary of the prevailing attitudes toward the company in key audiences.

• Any statistical information bearing on identity.

• Identity issues raised in executive interviews.

• Goals to be addressed by the new identity.

• Suggested management/naming reorganization, if applicable.

• Recommended changes in name, graphics and range of application needed to meet strategic goals.

---

for the identity program, although most of the time that need sells itself. You merely make clear what the client probably already suspects.

A Manner of Speaking. The manner in which you conduct the presentation can have a bearing on how easily your recommendations are accepted. Orchestrate slides or exhibits to lead the client to the very conclusion you've come to— that is, to make the client see the inevitability of your recommendations. The better you're able to summarize and interpret research findings, the more willing the client will be. In the words of one identity master, "If you build a strong rationale, people will be carried by your opinion, and the agreement will be carried by the rationale."

To prevent the possibility of missteps, some designers script their entire presentation, choosing language carefully and fielding questions only at the very end. Others rely on a thorough knowledge of the issues and arm themselves only with the briefest notes. You'll have to consider your relationship with the client to determine the best presentation style. Certainly, you should exude a good deal of confidence to counter any client

doubt and be able to show that there is sound reasoning behind every recommendation.

In preparing and delivering your presentation, remember that what you are about to show your clients may be very painful for them to see. No one likes to look at their warts, much less have them magnified by a slide projector across the end of a conference room. You need to be a diplomat and focus not on the negatives, but on the positive actions to be effected by the new identity program.

Some designers go so far as to present preliminary design directions at this meeting. For a large company with many applications, this will probably be premature—the designer simply will not have had the opportunity to seriously consider the full range of identity applications. However, a naming hierarchy and the use of a particular style of symbol or logotype might be recommended at this time.

For a smaller company with whom you have a more intimate rapport, a preliminary design might be useful, providing applications have been well considered. However, be forewarned that, since no agreement as to criteria has yet been reached, nor any production budget finalized or contract signed, the hours spent in developing a preliminary design may simply become lost time.

When the presentation has been completed, expect the client to mull over the recommendations for a few days. Clients will need time to discuss issues among themselves and perhaps take soundings from subordinates. Schedule a follow-up meeting in a week or so to discuss any changes in the recommendations. If the client is not ready then, you will have to wait; however, don't let him stall too long. It's important to keep the ball rolling. Issue a revised set of recommendations for his signature. This sign-off is important to be certain that everyone is working to the same set of ground rules. It also establishes a pattern of clear communication between you and the client—a pattern that could save thousands of dollars in misunderstandings later on. Make a practice of obtaining a written sign-off at the conclusion of each phase of identity development.

At this point, you can let the client know the approximate schedule for the remaining phases—how long design development can be expected to take, for example, or when all application and implementation will be completed. You might also outline working and approval procedures for those phases.

Having finished the enormous task of fact-finding and establishing criteria, you are at last ready to embark on the most exciting aspect of an identity program: design development.

Design Development

In an interview with Steven Heller in *Graphic Design in America* (Abrams, 1989), Paul Rand, a pioneer of identity design, borrowed from architect and visionary Le Corbusier: "If you don't build a thing right, it's going to cave in. And in a sense you can apply this philosophy to graphic design."

By the time you have reached the development phases of an identity project, you should have already laid a solid foundation for the design work to come. The information gathered in the research and interview phases will constantly shape ideas and provide direction during the design process; and the criteria established there will serve as constant reference points for gauging a design's appropriateness. Without such preparation, the entire identity system just might cave in.

If research is the foundation of the corporate identity process, design development is the superstructure. This section discusses aspects of design development such as name generation, the development and testing of the primary corporate identifier, ways to spark creativity in the design process, and how to present a new graphic identity to the client.

Basics of Design Development

The number of steps in the development phases of the identity process depends on the client's needs. Initial work will be exploratory, as you experiment and sketch out ideas; later, you will refine and finalize these initial concepts.

A massive identity overhaul might call for all the steps listed below; a mild spruce-up, only the last few:

- Developing a new company name.
- Developing a naming system that reflects how the company is organized.
- Developing visual identifier(s) appropriate to the nature of the business and its goals.
- Developing communications programs to introduce and explain the new identity.
- Applying and implementing the new identity across the entire company.

While each of these steps has its unique challenges, some considerations apply to the entire identity-building process. Perhaps the most important is appropriateness—that the name, graphic or identity application always be right for the company's line of business and management style, right for its audience and markets, and right in light of its culture and goals.

But appropriateness itself can be hard to determine. Sometimes our ideas about this quality are more influenced by our training and existing concepts than by the facts at hand—by what we have been conditioned to think is the "right" graphic symbol for a bank, for example, rather than by who the client is and what its needs are. It takes effort and keen awareness to cultivate freshness rather than generate the next generic symbol.

One way to avoid generic design is to keep focused on what is different about a client's business, what separates it from the competition. Another way is to be always pushing the creative envelope, always stretching the design process—and maybe the client's acceptance—toward unusual or innovative (and potentially riskier) solutions.

It's sad but true: Safe design solutions are generally also the most boring, and they seldom set the client apart. They may be scientifically tested and antiseptically safe, but they will become lost in the crowd. A designer sometimes has to explain this to clients, and encourage them to pursue their own uniqueness.

Another important quality in a graphic identity program is longevity. A name or graphic identifier should last long enough to bring the client to its business goals and beyond, and that may mean a decade or more. And yet, longevity should not be construed as permanence. To quote once more from Heller's interview with Paul Rand: "A good solution, in addition to being right, should have the potential for longevity. Yet I don't think we can design for permanence. One designs for function, for usefulness, rightness, beauty. Permanence is up to God."

Names

Although a name change can be a difficult and costly enterprise, and probably should be avoided if possible, companies sometimes do have good reason to change their names. A company needs a new name if its current name is:

- Limiting to strategic goals, or does not accurately convey the nature of the company's business.
- Outdated or perceived as stodgy or old-fashioned.
- Limiting to geographic or market expansion.
- Not unique or memorable.
- Too long or too difficult to pronounce.
- Conjuring negative associations, either by past business experience or because of emerging social trends.
- Being diluted by a recent merger or acquisition.

Because of the great number of company and product names in use today, finding a new company name is a process loaded with strategy. At the same time, it is immensely creative, drawing on both linguistic and psychological associations. Generally speaking, any name has to position the company in its markets, attract both customers and qualified personnel, be memorable and easy to pronounce, have positive verbal associations, and be legally protectable.

The first step in the naming process is to set down what strategic goals and criteria the new name will have to meet. Consider the name you are about to cast aside. What are its saving qualities? Its weaknesses? Where does it work, and why? Where and why *doesn't* it work? How will the new name help further business strategy?

Because the new name must work in any number of contexts, you will want to consider who will be its prime audiences and where they will be located. Will the name convey a positive meaning in regional, national and international markets? Does it sound like any foreign word that has negative associations?

Types of Names. Names fall into a few main categories. (Refer to page 7 for more on the categories of names.) Here we'll look at the benefits of three types: descriptive, initials, and fabricated or coined.

Descriptive names, such as United Parcel Service and Ford Motor Company, are those that verbally identify the nature of a company's business or its founder. They are especially useful where a name needs to convey quickly and clearly the nature of the company's business. Studies have shown that both consumers and shareholders prefer names with intrinsic meaning. Their major drawbacks are that they may become too generic and are, by their very nature, harder to legally protect.

Initials work best if they have been derived from a longer name with long-standing equity. IBM and GE would have been difficult names to promote, had not the well-known International Business Machines and General Electric names preceded them.

Fabricated, or coined, names can be created to specific criteria. Because certain coined names, such as Kodak and Xerox, have long-standing equity, you might be tempted to recommend them. They do have a certain modernity or a technological feel; they can work well for a narrow, nonconsumer audience; and they are useful in situations where a company is so diversified that no one de-

When Starting to Design, Remember:

• Employees, customers and investors all seem to prefer names and marks or symbols with obvious meaning.

• Logomarks with too many parts or that are too intricate will be less memorable and harder to reproduce than strong, simple marks.

• Logomarks that follow the latest design trend are usually doomed to an early death.

• Identity design strategy should be to constantly simplify and clarify.

• The best logomarks do not float in space but have some grounding reference point that hints at their placement.

• Watch out for logomarks that are derived from a certain product, service or industry; they, too, are doomed if the company should decide to diversify.

scriptive name can accurately convey all the parts. However, coined names also run the risk of being trendy and becoming dated. And since most fabricated names lack verbal or experiential associations, a lot of money must be spent to promote them until they achieve some audience awareness.

Probably the most successful names run a middle route between descriptive and fabricated names. They can be associative, derivative or allusive, suggesting the nature of the company's business or its positive attributes, while providing enough uniqueness to position the company and set it apart. Such a name can be memorable, attractive and wholly protectable: "Sunmaid," "Cat's Paw," "True Value."

Generating Names. Developing a name involves creative processes similar to developing a design solution. In the past, naming a company or product often followed the "Aha!" principle: Someone got a flash of inspiration. Such insight *is* possible, but it's more likely to occur if the mo-

```
Base Words/Phrases:

Trans            Function
Inter            Important
Intro            Merit
Smart            Source
Best             Venture
Excell           Value
Advantage        Fare
Post             Fair
Parcel           Efficient
Agent            Effective
Service (Serv)   Expert
Systems          Adept
Network (Net)    Skill
Prime            Craft
Class            Pro
Next             Professional
Send             Know
Excello          Knowledge
Excellens        Wise
Ex               Alert
Assignment       Bright
Task             Effort
```

```
Systems (s):

Systems/Source       SystemsServes
SystemsNet           SystemServ
SystemsWorks         SystemSystems
SystemsVantage       SystemPlus
SystemsCenter        SystemVentures
SystemsKnow          Systemax
SystemsServices
SystemServe
SystemsServe
```

Crosby Associates' name development for SystemaxNetwork began with brainstorming off a number of words and phrases related to the client's in-store parcel shipping service. The chain resulting from the word "systems" ended in what ultimately became the company's name: SystemaxNetwork.

ment is informed by research and analysis.

Developing a name might proceed something like this:

1. Do simple research.

2. Assemble group(s) for brainstorming and/or run computer name generations.

3. Evaluate names.

After reviewing the criteria and goals, start digging around for words that suggest or relate to the client's business. A dictionary or thesaurus will help, as will reference books such as collections of quotations or American slang words. You'll also want to check industry lists, available from trade associations, to see what names others in the field are already using.

Brainstorming is a good way to generate names to add to your list. It helps if the people involved have different backgrounds or different reference points for naming. The best people are bright, creative types who are also articulate; they can be members of the working committee, your associates, or trusted individuals from outside.

Assume the role of moderator, and brief the group as to criteria and goals. Then throw a few words, ideas or directions out for grabs. Write every name down on a blackboard or on pieces of paper that can be tacked up around the room for all to see. Get people acting on and bouncing off of each other's ideas. Keep going until participants begin to show signs of burn-out, usually within an hour or two.

Generating names by computer produces a lot of possibilities, too; however, few of them may have real meaning for the client. One popular name-generation software package allows you to specify the type of name needed. Then it generates names by building on linguistic patterns common to English verbs and nouns. You fine-tune these by selecting preferences or add another database of preferred words or syllables to obtain more or less descriptive meaning. The program can also check words for negative connotations in five languages.

Have a list of up to a thousand possibilities before you begin evaluating them against the established naming criteria. You'll cross some off immediately for obvious defects: they can't be pronounced; they're already taken; they're too contrived, too boring, or don't meet stated goals. In the next round, consider how accurately the name describes the company or its products and services; whether it has strong promotional capabilities; if it's catchy or memorable; and if it can be graphically interpreted. Repeat the process until maybe a few dozen names are left.

Discuss with the client the trimmed list of names, and reduce it by half. If there is a working committee, ask it to rank preferences and monitor testing. Check the best bets for meanings in other languages and for consumer preferences, and then test them against strategic goals.

Often, large corporations who change their names test them with focus groups and consumer surveys. Average citizens are asked questions like, "What does this name mean to you? What kind of image comes to mind? What kind of company does it sound like? What kind of products do you think a company with this name might make? Which of the names we've talked about is your favorite? Your least favorite? Why?"

Names for small businesses are not as likely to be tested. Their owners tend to trust their own instincts. Moreover, since testing can be an expensive process, their budgets simply may not allow it. In such cases, use your own judgment and the opinions of your usual sounding boards.

When you have a handful of bona fide candidates ranked in order of preference, someone should check to make sure they aren't already owned by someone else. Some lawyers make a specialty of trademark and patent searches. If the client can afford it, retain these services to research a name before a lot of design time is invested in it. Otherwise, contact the Patent and Trademark Office of the U.S. Department of Commerce (Washington, D.C. 20231) for information about registering trade names.

Design Strategies

Once the question of naming has been settled (if indeed it was raised), you're ready to approach a graphic design.

Logomarks. Many clients and designers assume that a company has to have a symbol. But this is not the case. Increasingly designers are finding that individual trademarks have all but lost their meaning in a sea of symbols. So, one of the earliest considerations for the identity designer is whether the client is better served by a logotype, a symbolic mark, or a combination of the two. (For more on this, see pages 7-9.)

A symbolic identifier is ideal if the client is a small company with one line of business (a typing service), or if its several businesses are easily conveyed with one graphic image (a forest products company). A symbol is also the most direct way to identify a company whose name immediately suggests a figure, as do names like Bell Telephone, International Red Cross and Dutch Boy paints.

Many designers prefer working with a company's name alone to develop a distinctive signature. This means developing a name-based mark, not just by selecting a typeface, but by altering or augmenting letterforms in such a way as to enhance meaning without sacrificing legibility.

A company's name is, after all, the primary expression of its identity. A name-based mark reinforces that perception. Using the name alone may also offer the advantage of standing out in a crowd where generic symbols abound. And by choosing a name-based mark, you avoid the problem common to symbol-and-logotype identities: Despite established graphic standards, the client sometimes splits the logotype and symbol apart, using each in separate and inappropriate circumstances.

If your client's existing identity has established value, you'll want to be sure to identify and retain any key visual elements—those forms which have made it stick in the mind of the viewer. Strong continuity is important here, both to sharpen existing loyalties and to preserve value established through use.

Typography. Typography, of course, is a primary medium for a company's visual communication; so, as you proceed through identity development, keep in mind all the ways the client will

SYSTEMAX NETWORK

Some exploratory logotypes developed by Crosby Associates in its search for an identity for Systemax-Network.

systemaxnetwork

The final SystemaxNetwork logomark.

use the new identity in printed communications. For example, is it more important for the house style to be serviceable (for a lot of printed communications) or unique (for a few attention-getting applications)? Should the face be serif or sans serif? Is there an advantage to combining the two? To using two different serif or sans serif styles for different applications (one for annual reports, say, and one for promotions)? Selecting the right one is all a matter of appropriateness.

Most identity systems use one or two type families in a limited number of weights—Futura Light, Medium and Extra Bold, for example, or Times Roman and Times Bold. Too many typographic variations, or a mix of several typefaces, will create a chaotic, unstructured look and dilute any sense of corporate style.

Typography can draw attention to a company's identity or to its printed communications. After that, it should disappear. Overlapping letterforms, unusually tight or loose space, or a wild mix of typefaces may attract the eye, but they will sabotage clear communication.

Color. Books have been written about the psychology of color and its importance in human response. However, most identity designers take even "scientific" color theories with a grain of salt. Of primary consideration are their client's needs and how color can help resolve them.

Color can evoke emotion by communicating certain attributes and thus infusing an identity with vitality. It can help to build a lasting identity by attracting attention, facilitating recognition and stimulating recall.

Through consistent application, color can also be used to link divisions and brands to the parent company. Color is most useful in an identity program, however, for its ability to differentiate a company from its competitors, for example, or sister operating units from one another. So, in considering a corporate color, you will first have to assess whether there is a real need for color differentiation, and where.

Many identity programs specify one company color and use it with black for copy in print applications. Defining a second corporate color increases printing costs, and some companies are not willing to go the added expense. Still, some designers do specify two-color logomarks, or they use colored papers to provide the feel of a second color. For accuracy, corporate colors are always specified in the Pantone™ Matching System (PMS) or other readily available color matcher.

Selecting a corporate color does have its pitfalls. Those colors most comfortable to the client are also likely to be those that are most widely used and thus most generic: red, blue and green. Moreover, selecting a shade of one of these popular colors as a differentiating tactic may be an exercise in futility. For most audiences, red is red, no matter where it appears on the color wheel. Similarly, IBM is blue—any blue, though, of course, officially it is only one specific blue.

Programs that are too rigid about color become numbing very quickly, as the company color begins to appear everywhere. Corporate colors are therefore best limited to corporate materials, where they help define corporate style and signal a corporate communication. In other applications where liveliness is a factor—advertising, sales promotion, even interior design—a one-color rule can be a real killer. In such circumstances, exercise restraint and have the signature color appear as an accent, perhaps, or in the logomark alone.

As a final check, especially for international applications, consider possible negative or unsuitable cultural connotations. White may mean purity in Europe and North America but in India, white is the color of mourning. Because color can mean many things to many people, the audience should always be a prime consideration in color selection.

Design Exploration

A client who has little understanding of the design process may ask for a logomark or letterhead design to be produced overnight. But the informed design of an effective corporate identifier can be a lengthy process, involving a few weeks to a few months of active exploration. Take as much time as you need to get it right; otherwise the quality— and effectiveness—of the whole identity program

About Symbol Design . . .

In developing symbols, avoid overworked images such as single capital letters, stars, the globe, etc., unless you can bring to bear an entirely fresh interpretation. Here are some points to keep in mind while developing a symbol identifier. Symbol designs should be:

- Highly memorable.
- Unique within the client's industry.
- Flexible for present and future applications.
- Effective in black and white as well as color.
- Reproducible in all sizes from a few millimeters to huge billboards, by any designer.
- Reproducible in a variety of materials, on different surfaces, for a range of applications.
- Adaptable to laser and dot matrix printing.
- Translatable to other languages and cultures, if necessary.
- Conducive to animation, if televised advertising is a possibility.

will suffer. The real danger lies in developing a logomark alone, rather than a solution that will work as a systematic identity. As each design is developed, you need to be able to visualize it in its full range of applications—not always an easy task.

In evaluating the graphic possibilities, keep in mind your responsibility to your client. Too often identity programs fail because the designer forgot about appropriateness and delivered a fabulously stylish but short-lived solution, or one that was calculated more to make the designer look good than to meet the client's needs.

But also guard against delivering the expected. Often the expected or commonplace solution fails because it is neither unique nor memorable. Look for an answer that goes a little

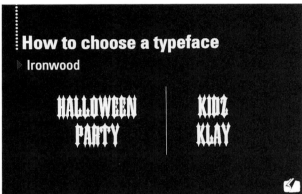

To illustrate a point about typography and appropriateness, Lynne Garell, corporate type marketing manager at Adobe Systems, set phrases conveying two different ideas in two widely disparate typefaces. Designers can use similar techniques to test the appropriateness of their own type specs.

beyond the ordinary. If you don't, you're working against the whole basis of projecting a unique identity.

Finally, beware the easy solution. The obvious answer may be *too* obvious; it may be a visual cliché or totally lacking in individuality. True, the seed of the solution is sometimes obvious, but it can take a lot of time and effort to bring it to perfection. Don't be afraid to spend it.

Coming Up With Ideas. Designers use many methods to come up with ideas for a graphic identity. Where two or more designers work on design development, they all should start with the same brief, based on the research findings. There will usually follow some kind of discussion of possible directions, and perhaps some brainstorming to shake loose any preconceptions. Then they go back to their separate spaces and work up their ideas. Such multiminded idea development produces a larger pool of possibilities. Granted, not all the ideas will be good, but there will ultimately be more of them to explore, and the competitive dynamic can push design quality upward.

After a week or two, the designers come back and discuss their ideas. Their sketches, however rough, are put up on the wall and evaluated against the agreed-upon criteria. They will attack, defend, debate and eliminate — a worthwhile process when you consider how the real world looks at any graphic identifier. The inferior and unsuitable ideas will quickly disappear, leaving a few to be further pursued. Ideally, one to three solutions are eventually left for final consideration.

Sparking creativity, especially when working alone, can be challenging. If you're an independent designer, you need to use everything at your disposal to support yourself in the search for the great idea — your favorite music, your lucky marker, a round of deep breathing, whatever. And you'll also need some self-discipline and a little hard work.

One way to start is by writing each of your criteria on a piece of paper and hanging it on the wall of your workspace. Develop a mass of symbols or logomarks for each attribute. Be sure to include different types of marks (figurative, ab-

Sources of Inspiration

Some designers get started by reviewing all the criteria and then taking a long walk; some go to the movies; some meditate. Give yourself whatever you need to keep your thinking fresh and alive.

Go to an art museum or gallery, or browse through some art history books. Look at other types of design—architecture, furnishings, crafts. Mining design annuals and collections of identity solutions can be a good place to start, but be forewarned. Sometimes, instead of gaining insight and understanding, you may be tempted to copy an existing design, doing neither your client nor the original designer any justice.

Some designers maintain clip files of things that catch their eye. Such image banks might include the detail of a door molding, a photo of a fantastic garden, the pattern for a patchwork quilt, or any other interesting visual. It can be a clipping from a magazine or newspaper, a doodle or a sketch. It can be ideas developed for myriad other projects and never used. All are grist for the mill.

stract and typographic). Take marks from each attribute, or of each type, and combine them.

Some designers believe sketching is best accomplished with pen or pencil. Others sketch by cutting up colored papers and so work out color problems at the same time. Some use amberlith and a matte knife, or a computer. Cutting and pasting with a photocopier is a great help in this process, and can save hours of drawing time.

Probably the best way is to start with thumbnails. Fill pages. Trace typefaces from specimen books to get a feel for how your symbols will work with different typefaces. Experiment with letter spacing and type placement. Use typing correction fluid to lighten designs, black marker to strengthen them. Trace or cut out parts of one design and add them to another.

Although sketching lends itself to symbol solutions, don't overlook the possibility that the ideal mark for your client may be a logotype alone. Pursue all types of solutions during the initial phases of design exploration: symbols, logotypes and combination forms. Two separately developed ideas for a logotype and a symbol just may come together to create one powerful identity.

If you use a computer for design, you can save a lot of time by working directly on the screen. You can produce variations quickly without much handwork and can explore basic applications for your designs. Images can be evaluated and rejected as they are created, or stored for later review. Some designers create image banks on their computers and mine them for every project.

As more design offices equip themselves with computers, design and layout programs will keep getting better. The only danger in using such technology is letting it become more than a tool for creativity. No computer program, however sophisticated, can match the raw creativity of a real live designer.

Finalizing Your Design. Constantly evaluating solutions against the criteria established and agreed upon with the client quickly weeds out unlikely prospects. When you have maybe a dozen possibilities left, begin testing them in thumbnails of stationery or other applications to see how well they work. You can even take this process further and develop full-size trials of the most likely designs.

There should remain only a handful of "best bet" designs in the running. These should be subjected to thorough, systematic exploration to determine the ideal color, proportion and placement of each element in the design. Then see how the solution fits layouts for stationery, business cards, packaging, vehicles, and other intended applications.

Decide how many sketches and/or solutions you are going to show the client and when. Some designers show no exploratory work at all, saving everything for the final client presentation. Others like to bring clients into the design process by showing them work in progress. These designers feel client input keeps them in sync with client preferences, saving time that might otherwise be spent on solutions the client will never accept. It lets clients feel involved with the identity design process, instilling a proprietary feeling from the start. And it clearly shows clients how much thought, time and energy go into identity design development.

If you go this route, be sure to show a client only those sketches you feel represent viable solutions, or she may fall in love with something inappropriate. To maintain control of such early presentations, be sure you can discuss the relative merits of each idea.

If your style is to present your ideas as finished designs, decide beforehand how many solutions you are going to comp up and present to the client. Do this by comparing your best bets against one another and ordering them by how well they meet the established criteria. Consider which lend themselves to the widest variety of application, and which will exhibit the greatest natural consistency in application.

Testing Your Solution. It is debatable whether a new graphic identity should be tested somehow before being embraced by the corporation. The nub of the conflict is illustrated by a story about a designer, charged with implementing what would become one of the most successful corporate identities of all time, who tested his solution by showing it around the company. Fully 75 percent of the people who saw it didn't like it. The designer, however, was convinced that it was right. "What do they know?" he reportedly asked. "They are dealing in history, in what has transpired. I am dealing in the future."

Whenever a new identity is tested by showing

Some of the first pencil sketches made by John Evans of Sibley/Peteet Design, Dallas, for the Padre Staples shopping mall, located on the Gulf coast of Texas.

Further explorations, executed in marker.

A dozen of the forty or so marker sketches Sibley/Peteet showed to the client. In this first round, individually mounted sketches were spread across the conference table. Although the process can take several rounds of picking and choosing, in this case, the client made a first-round selection that was taken to final art.

Final art for the Padre Staples Mall graphic identity. The version with the leaf detail is used for large applications, such as signage.

Padre Staples Mall

Some of the logotype and symbol ideas developed concurrently by Sibley/Peteet Design for Sweatyme, a manufacturer of fitness wear and accessories. All were shown to the client.

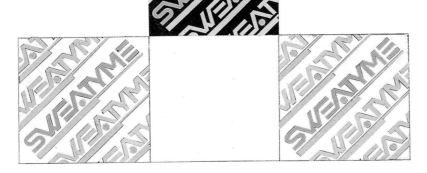

Color logotype and packaging trial comps for Sweatyme's fitness accessories, as presented for client approval.

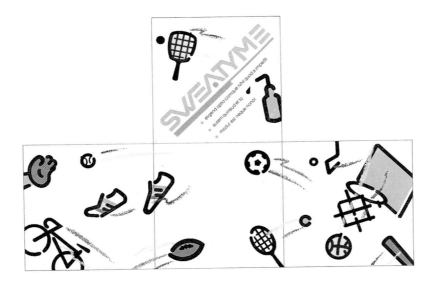

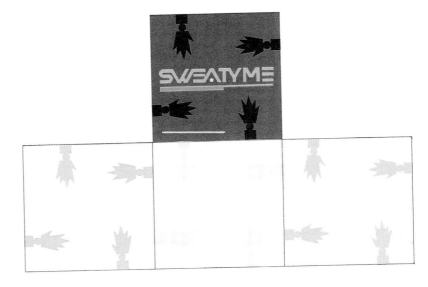

The comps selected by the client.

it to focus groups, client representatives or other interested parties, the viewers will judge it from their own preconceived notions about what a particular kind of company or product is supposed to look like. Designing *solely* from such input almost always leads to boring, predictable identities. And acting from the past won't move a company or its graphic identity where it should go in the future.

Clients with small, entrepreneurial companies don't often ask for consumer testing. They know what they like when they see it and, if the relationship warrants, will trust their designer's recommendations. However, some clients like the kind of scientific reassurance that testing provides. And for those clients, you may have to back up your solution with some positive statistics.

Some research firms use sophisticated electronic devices to track viewer eye movement and measure the appeal of designs. Many others use focus groups and surveys to tally consumer response. Unfortunately, only large corporate clients with significant budgets may be willing and able to hire outside researchers. Other clients may expect their designers to provide this service.

One relatively inexpensive way to do so is to organize a focus group—a meeting at which you gauge the reaction of a half-dozen or so people who have an interest in your client's type of business. The group may be screened for any factors you feel are pertinent. In an informal, relaxed session, participants are briefed on the subject and then shown the designs, one at a time.

Ask leading questions to bring out the group's opinions. Watch the participants' reactions and listen to their comments. You should know enough about the participants to be able to assess and weigh their prejudices about your client's business. Attempt to gauge whether the interviewees are answering truthfully or merely saying what they think is expected of them.

You may choose to do some informal testing regardless of whether the client asks for it. One identity master often tested his designs on his wife or his daughter, his plumber, his accountant—whoever happened to be available at the time. Similarly, many designers feel showing a po-

tential solution to a nondesigner can quickly bring the designer back to earth. If the secretary or pizza delivery boy thinks your wonderfully inventive "W" logomark looks like a plane crashing to earth, you know it's time to go back to the drawing board.

Legalities

The legal aspects of a graphic identity are based both in its being a piece of intellectual property—a product of skill and imagination—and in its having worth in the marketplace. Like any trademark, it can be bought and sold, stolen or infringed upon.

Before selling a mark to a client, it is your responsibility to be sure it can be registered. Some large design firms have on-staff researchers, to check and cross-check the names and logomarks they develop to see if they are already in use. Others use outside consultants.

If your design derives from or closely resembles an existing mark, have its availability verified for applicable markets by a trademark expert. A trademark lawyer or agent can perform such a search, using computerized services. Names are more likely to be a problem than symbols, which can be slightly modified and still be legal. If the name or mark is owned but not in use and you want to obtain the rights, the process can be expensive and time-consuming. Be certain the expense is worthwhile—and the client can afford it—before going this route.

Protecting the Mark. Graphic identities are protected in two ways: as trade names, which identify companies, and as trademarks, the devices that identify products and services. Technically, it is not necessary to register trademarks at all, since they are protected by common law. Moreover, a name or design has to be actually in use before rights can be established. Still, registering a mark with the U.S. Patent and Trademark Office, and foreign registering bodies if necessary, will establish ownership from a specific date and legally retain exclusive use. (This is more likely to be a concern of larger, corporate clients or government organizations than smaller

To Protect Your Client's Logomark:

• Carefully and consistently implement it, without modification, across the range of applications.

• Typographically distinguish it from running text via color, typeface or type style.

• Always follow the mark or name with a generic identifier that clearly positions the name as an adjective, not a noun or verb; never use the name as a plural noun.

• Use the accepted indicators ® (for marks of all types) or ™ (which can be used from the start, with or without registration) in all applications.

• Sign, date and keep all drawings and original art used in developing the mark.

• Recommend that your client register the mark in all countries where it will be used, and in all applicable product/service categories.

Such precautions are necessary because, if infringement is discovered later, the way the logomark has been used will be important in any legal action. Consistent use and application will indicate the client's clear intent to protect the logomark as intellectual property, and will preclude any infringer's claims of ignorance.

---

companies, local businesses or nonprofit groups.) For more information, contact the Patent and Trademark Office, U.S. Department of Commerce, Washington, D.C. 20231. (For more on how to protect your client's logomark, see the sidebar directly above.)

Designer's Rights. Once you sell a graphic identity to a client, you lose all rights to it—unless you have specifically reserved certain rights in your contract. Sometimes designers retain all rights in their designs per contract with their clients. (Similarly, anyone you hire to execute part of the identity work—lettering, illustration, typography, etc.—will have to pass rights of ownership to you or your client.) Without such contractual agreement, your client, as the owner of the mark's copyright or trademark registration, will retain full control.

If you aren't the copyright holder, what rights should you keep? Not holding the rights to use a piece for publicity or self-promotion could prevent you from entering your work into competitions, especially those that become published as design annuals. It might also prevent your work from being included in textbooks or designer's guides like this one.

To protect your own interests in your work, your contract or work agreement with the client must be clear as to just what rights you will sell to the client and what rights you will retain. Most clients who establish copyright ownership of their corporate identities do not object to the designer's retaining rights for self-promotion or publicity purposes, nor could they likely bar the marks' inclusion in the editorial coverage of newspapers or magazines that report on the graphic design scene. On the other hand, they may not want their marks appearing in other types of publications, such as textbooks and design compendiums. If you sense that your client might be sensitive about even news coverage, you'd better clear all such uses in writing, right at the start. Generally, designers retain all sketches and other developmental material directly related to the final mark, but some clients do insist on purchasing these. Unless specifically purchased by the client, any other developmental materials—such as exploratory sketches not related to the final design, rejected ideas, or unselected comps—remain your property.

Final Comps

Comping sample applications of your proposed graphic identity is an important part of finalizing your design. Beyond supplying a context for visualization, comping allows both you and your client to see that the identity solution really works. Comping, even more than placement sketching, brings your design to life, making the solution tangible and real.

As the centerpiece of an identity system, the new logomark is obviously the most important piece of the program to comp. It should be large, by itself, and as accurate as possible. The other comps you prepare will depend on the size of the client's business and how many items final implementation will include. Usually five or six significant applications are enough to show the client how the new identity will work—stationery and business cards, signage, vehicles, and a few print applications, such as advertising or sales materials. Comps for a restaurant identity should include matches, menus and take-out containers; for a dry cleaner include bill heads and garment bags or hanger covers. Prepare comps and applications of as many separate logomark solutions as you intend to show the client. (See pages 46-47.)

The comps themselves can take many forms. For his presentation to the Together Center (see pages 84-87), David Butler made a black-and-white print of a symbol cut from amberlith, then sketched in colored pencil its application to a stationery package. Jeff Larson comped up stationery for Northwest Passage (see pages 76-82) with custom transfers of the logomark applied to the recommended letterhead stock. Or you can use colored press-on films, cut paper mounted on board, or marker drawings. Computers are excellent tools for creating lifelike comps, often at a lower cost than traditional production methods. This is one of the major reasons many designers invest in computers. Also, try to demonstrate special printing techniques. For example, to indicate blind embossing, cut the shape to be embossed from the recommended paper and affix it in position on the comped letterhead.

Whatever method you choose, consider which materials you feel comfortable with, the time and budget available, and your client's ability to visualize. But remember that the more a comp looks like the real thing, the easier it is to visualize—and to sell.

Presenting Comps to the Client. Probably no designer alive doesn't have at least a small case of nerves when showing a proposed corporate identity solution to a client for the first time. Bolster your confidence by careful preparation. (See the tips for a client presentation on pages 33-35.) Outline or script everything you plan to say. Practice your presentation to gain confidence; visualize every step going smoothly and successfully. Keep in mind that the client is excited and eager to see your designs; you can capitalize on this receptivity. The result will be a presentation that addresses the objectives and shows your work in its best light.

Take control of a presentation from the start, and you will have your audience exactly where you want it at all times. By now you have a pretty good idea what your client does or doesn't understand about identity design. Give her what she needs to hear about how your proposed identity will work for her. Make your approach systematic and orderly, so she can simply listen and follow.

A good way to open your presentation is by reviewing the objectives that your identity design is supposed to meet—the agreed-upon criteria. You might also want to review what was revealed in earlier research. This focuses everyone's attention on the real issues at hand. Never assume that the client remembers what was reported before; she is a busy person with many things on her mind. Besides, months may have elapsed since she signed off on the criteria.

How many choices you want to offer your client is up to you. Some identity designers show only one solution and present it as the best; they feel that allowing a client, especially a client committee, to pick and choose from among possible identities only courts disaster. If your client has a poor design sense and a history of wanting to act as art director to your work, showing several alternatives can be a mistake. She may demand more

Presentation Dramatics

Some designers like to dramatize a presentation by having the proposed logomark cast in stone, metal or even chocolate. This psychological ploy somehow makes the identity tangible and real. Clients may find it easier to buy your solution simply because it is so tangible. It's a bit of show business, but it works.

exploration after deciding to mix and match existing bits of designs. If you're working with a committee, showing several options may result in a gridlock if one person insists on Design A and another insists on Design B.

On the other hand, many people find it easier to settle on one solution if they can first reject one or two others. In such cases, show one solution that is obviously stronger than the others. It should have your clear recommendation and absolutely meet the established criteria. Along with your first choice, present one or two alternatives or have them with you as back-ups. (Even a client who loves your recommended solution may ask, "What else did you think of?")

Should you show sketches at a presentation? Some designers never do; they feel it undermines their professional image. Instead, they show only finished, highly polished comps. Other designers think showing sketches helps the client see where their solution is coming from. If you want to show some of your sketches and roughs, you can bring them along or put them on slides. Showing developmental materials allows you to recap the development process, leading the client where you want to go: to the obvious conclusion of your recommended design. Explain why each design was rejected, how your final logomark meets the established criteria, and why it works best in comparison with those you rejected. Finally, present your solution(s) and several applications.

Selling Your Design. The most convincing selling point for a proposed graphic identity is that it clearly meets the established criteria. Even a highly inventive or daring solution can be sold when it is shown to be rational and viable. As one identity designer puts it, clients don't buy an identity design; they buy a rationale.

Sometimes it is necessary to help your clients buy into a new level of vision and stretch their thinking about graphic identity—particularly if your proposal is a radical departure from the client's expectations. (See pages 15-17 for more on handling client expectations.) Some clients are more comfortable with innovation than others. Know your client and your client's business before deciding how much you can push the creative envelope with your designs.

Ultimately, clients have to feel comfortable with the identity they buy. If a client is in any way uncomfortable about the solution—especially if she feels forced into that solution—she may buy it but won't be happy with it. And an unhappy client is a lost client.

When Barney Tabach, proprietor of Schaffer's Bridal & Formalwear, was running out of garment bags, he asked his neighbor, designer John Sayles, if he could come up with a nicer design. Sayles knew that Tabach was using a variety of collateral all with unrelated designs. He took the initiative and developed a whole new identity for Tabach's shop on spec, comping up not only a new garment bag, but a letterhead, hangtags, and a hatbox. Sayles' final comps for client approval reflect revisions made after the logotype was finalized. They were created full scale, using markers and cut paper. Sayles' original logotype (top) went through a number of incarnations to accommodate his client's wishes to make it more feminine and to include more of the shop's name (second from top). By the third trial (second from bottom), however, both the client and the designer realized the mark had lost much of its original impact. The final logomark (bottom) represents an effective compromise.

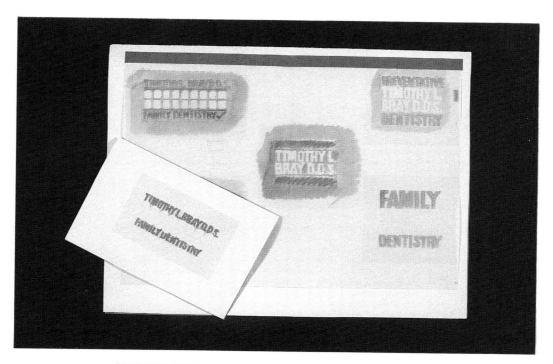

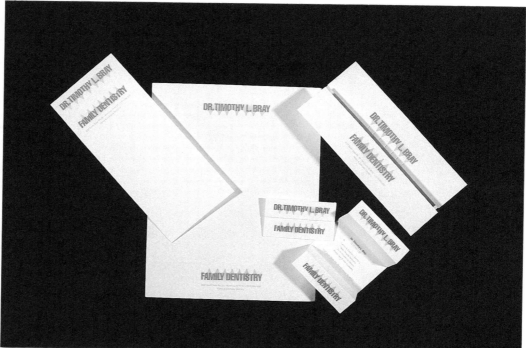

Tim Gant, of Held & Diedrich Design, used colored pencils to comp his witty ideas for a dentist's stationery. The printed version is embossed and scored, giving the design real "bite"!

These two logomark possibilities, and the ones shown on pages 58-59, were presented by Midnight Oil Studios to the Original Sports Saloon for their consideration. The client chose the logomark shown on page 59 for further development.

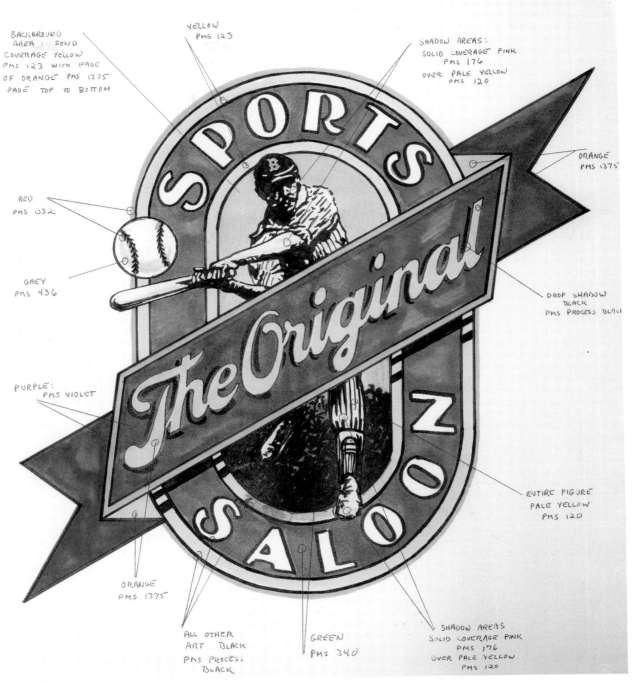

BACKGROUND AREA: SOLID COVERAGE YELLOW PMS 123 WITH FADE OF ORANGE PMS 1375 FADE TOP TO BOTTOM

YELLOW PMS 123

SHADOW AREAS: SOLID COVERAGE PINK PMS 176 OVER PALE YELLOW PMS 120

ORANGE PMS 1375

RED PMS 032

GREY PMS 436

DROP SHADOW BLACK PMS PROCESS BLACK

PURPLE: PMS VIOLET

ENTIRE FIGURE PALE YELLOW PMS 120

ORANGE PMS 1375

ALL OTHER ART BLACK PMS PROCESS BLACK

GREEN PMS 340

SHADOW AREAS SOLID COVERAGE PINK PMS 176 OVER PALE YELLOW PMS 120

Midnight Oil Studios submitted four logomark comps to its client, the Original Sports Saloon; each was a large, highly refined colored marker drawing. The client liked the oval format with the baseball player (above) so much that the project was expanded to include three more versions, each using this basic format — one each for football, basketball, and hockey. The logos were eventually used for a variety of marketing purposes, from architectural graphics to direct-mail postcards. (The other comps that were submitted are shown on the previous two pages.)

Application and Implementation

The final stage of a corporate identity project begins with developing standards for the new graphic identity to be applied to all of a company's visual communications; it ends as those standards are used to produce new communications materials.

Systematic, consistent application is the most important part of a corporate identity program. A strong corporate identity, haphazardly applied, will be less effective than a weak identity applied with diligence. One of the most common reasons companies call for an identity review is because a perfectly good mark has been used inconsistently.

Regardless of whether you will personally oversee the complete implementation of the corporate identity you have designed, you will want to address how application standards will be documented in an identity manual.

Establishing a Plan

Application and implementation of a new corporate identity is by far the longest phase of the corporate identity process. The time needed varies according to the size of the company and the number of applications involved. Expect it to take at least a few months for a smaller company and as long as a few years for a large corporation.

This phase is so time-consuming because you must develop what is essentially a new design solution for every visual communication your client uses, or is likely to use: business papers and computer forms, calling cards and catalogs, price lists, sales materials, buildings and trucks. Then as identity standards are established, the project moves into implementation. Stationery and forms are printed; vehicles are repainted; new signs are ordered, fabricated and installed. You must plan and proof each of these applications, which are produced by an outside supplier. These steps, too, eat up time.

Inexperienced designers sometimes try to rush the application process. But instant design solutions are seldom effective, and a designer needs time to reflect, experiment and compare while applying a new graphic identity. The object is not to get the job done as quickly as possible, but to create a graphic communications system that unifies as well as identifies.

Project management holds the key. If an application course is carefully plotted, production will flow more smoothly, and supplier rush charges will be avoided.

First, consider the big picture. Figure how many separate application solutions are needed, and which ones can be combined into one simplified approach. You may be able to develop one set of standards for all 8½-by-11-inch forms, for example. Allow time to research and develop each application, as well as to review all of the applications together. Some designers don't send the first items off to press until they've at least sketched out the whole program. This can save money—and face—by preventing items from being printed before they have been tested against the entire system.

In scheduling, also factor in the amount of time various suppliers need to get specified materials, fabricate the new identity pieces, and deliver them to your client. Set priorities for development and production based on both your client's priorities and the suppliers' needs. Consider, too, your client's current inventories, and aim to meet the usual schedule for replacing stationery, forms, and other consumable items. When are facilities due to be refurbished? What is the turnover in vehicle fleets? Should trucks be painted or fitted with decals? Bear in mind that it may take years to replace all of the stationery, forms, packages and shippers for a large company if the attrition process, which is by far the most economical, is used.

The Client Connection. Project management at this phase may also include coordinating and controlling any application or implementation the client may take in-house. If your client has an in-house design department, or if your own capabilities are too limited to meet the demands of a large application/implementation program, you may have to hire and/or brief other designers, oversee standards development, and review the application results.

At this point, management may need to be reminded of the importance of a well-orchestrated identity, vigilantly applied. Their commitment should include standards development and application, as well as the careful maintenance of those standards throughout the life of the identity program, which may continue long after the designer has left the scene.

The client must understand that graphic identity is not a static decorator touch but a living entity to be managed. Many companies spend a lot of time and money devising a new graphic identity, then fail to follow through with effective management of all identity materials. The result is a hodgepodge of graphic communications that project an inconsistent image and undercut strategic and communications efforts—possibly the same problem that caused them to examine their graphic identity in the first place.

Management's commitment can be measured

by their spoken and written endorsement as well as by an adequate budget. Ideally, in a large corporation, management will empower an individual with authority and provide a budget that will enable him to effectively oversee the identity process across the whole organization. This will ensure the clout needed for implementation to continue and succeed. Some identity designers say that without this in-house manager, the identity program has a very slim chance at success.

Some larger corporations will already have a design manager who ensures the new identity is implemented according to form. Even if there is no design manager per se, there should be someone at the client company who continues the function of design liaison. While not necessarily a designer, this person should understand design and the objectives of the new identity program.

In a large corporation particularly, a design manager can be an invaluable ally in gaining the ear of top management during the implementation process. At times, effective application is only possible when the corporation's top executive takes a personal interest. For this reason, the design manager should be someone in the managing director's or president's office, with direct access to the top.

If there is no design manager, or if, in a small business, the client-owner is not able to take the job in hand, you will have to take on the dual tasks of developing applications and monitoring implementation. Some designers prefer to assume the latter role anyway and so maintain a long-term relationship with the client. Others design basic identifiers and applications only and then become consultants, overseeing applications done by the client or reviewing them after the fact.

Whoever performs these functions, someone must develop the channels by which information about the new identity program will reach all levels of employees. In large corporations, where there are often widely flung operations and interdepartmental rivalries, this can be a real challenge. The designer or design liaison must defuse destructive rivalries and promote the new identity as a unifying force. Component parts of a large company must be encouraged to see themselves as vital parts of the same whole, united in common goals.

Designing identity applications can be a fairly straightforward process. The comps approved by the client at the final presentation meeting form the basis of the process. These key pieces—logomark, stationery, advertising, architectural and vehicle signage, whatever—set the tone for the other graphic solutions needed to bring all of the client's communications into the new corporate identity system. Use them as models as you begin placement sketches for other applications.

Whether you are new to identity projects or an old hand, don't assume you know how your client's communications interface with the real world. Talk to the people who actually use them—the marketers who use promotion pieces, the warehouse personnel who know about digitized labels and multiuse shipping cartons. Check with the post office for the latest regulations on envelope design; discuss the letterhead with the secretaries who will follow your typing guidelines. Getting such input grounds your solutions in practical, real-world problems and saves costly reprinting to correct mistakes later on.

The strategic criteria established at the beginning of the project continue to serve as touchstones for applying the new identity.

• Does the design accurately represent the company and its goals?

• Does it distinguish the company from its competition?

• Does the design convey the company's unique personality?

• Is it visually consistent with other items in the identity program?

• Does it meet stated identity goals in a consistent and logical manner?

Using this approach, establish standards for applying the new identity medium by medium: stationery, calling cards and forms; advertising and sales promotion; consumer and warehouse packaging; architectural and vehicular signage. (A more complete list of possible applications is in "Manuals and Guidelines," pages 64-70.)

If your role is as a consultant monitoring the in-house application of the new identity, the process will be much the same. Your presentation comps will serve as models for all designers working on the project. Your input here will take the form of reviewing each new application for appropriateness and consistency, verifying that it meets stated communications goals. It's a good idea to do these reviews with the designers present, so you can offer pointers, hear their concerns and discuss alternatives.

Getting user input — from in-house designers, outside studios, ad agencies, packaging converters, printers and other interested parties — not only keeps the identity system in line with real-world issues, it brings users into the process, and so fosters enthusiasm for the program and a willingness to maintain identity standards.

Manuals and Guidelines

The classic format for corporate identity manuals is a set of thick loose-leaf binders, the covers silk-screened with the corporation's identifier. But what form your client's manual should take depends on the number of applications in the program, the number of copies needed, and the client's budget. Large standards manuals are meant to manage numerous and varied communications pieces. They work well when a large, decentralized corporation has many applications, produced at many different locations. And corporate customers tend to like them, not only for their content, but because they offer reassuring, tangible evidence of the corporate identity program they have purchased.

For smaller businesses with only a few applications, however, identity manuals are not usually necessary. More to the point are graphics guidelines — what one designer calls "an identity user's manual." These are the written standards that allow anyone to produce graphic communications in keeping with the corporate identity program. A more detailed discussion of each of these reference tools follows.

Corporate Standards Manual. For a large corporation, the graphic standards manual is the bible of corporate identity and is an absolute necessity for identity management. It forms a visible, enduring statement of a company's policy toward identity management for all those who come in contact with it.

Still, even the most comprehensive manuals can't guarantee that a graphic identity will always be correctly implemented. Manuals often can't go into the detail necessary to address every application situation that might possibly arise. Rather, they put forth both the spirit and the letter of identity application, and so ease implementation.

Toward this end, most identity manuals include a message from the corporation's CEO on page one. This letter explains the what and why of the new graphic identity, who has to abide by it, and management's clear commitment to it. (It also helps to have the CEO repeat this message in person at every possible opportunity until implementation is complete.)

You will usually write the rest of the text in the identity manual, because you know the system best. In addition to describing the pictured applications and supplying specifications for papers, typography, and the exact placement of type and logomark on stationery and other documents, you will also explain why each standard has been established as it has.

Make no assumptions about your audience. It is not uncommon for a standards manual to read like a design primer with discussions of, for example, the subtle balance achieved by the placement of the logomark, how the recommended white space around a headline makes it easier to read, or how different sizes and weights of type create an editorial hierarchy within a training manual or report. Such details are needed for the many non-designers who may influence the style and form of your client's communications, and whose interest in maintaining standards may not be as keen as your own.

Including your design rationales in the manual will help any designers who may work for your client in the future come to grips with what it means to follow standards. Many designers not involved with corporate design on a daily basis see

Who Gets a Copy of the Identity Manual?

A large corporation may need a few hundred copies of its graphic standards manual to cover all bases; a small business may only need one or two sets of guidelines. Here's a list of potential recipients for full or partial sets of graphic standards:

• Top management (full sets as trophies for owner, president, CEO, board members, operations managers).

• Identity manager(s).

• Communications officers.

• In-house designers.

• Advertising/promotion/marketing personnel.

• Production departments.

• Public relations personnel.

• Publications personnel.

• Administrative assistants/secretaries/typing or word processing pool.

• Divisional managers.

• Purchasing officers.

• Outside designers doing regularly contracted work.

• Ad agencies.

• Major suppliers such as printers, engravers, and packaging converters.

• Sign fabricators/vehicle painters.

• Members of the working committee.

---

graphic standards as a set of limiting rules that stop up their creative juices. But standards are in fact only parameters expressing the corporation's need to project a consistent identity. Good design and fresh thinking are what bring graphic standards to life, and your manual should encourage both of these.

At the same time, the design of the manual itself should reflect its position as a working document. It should also reflect the personality of the client company, rather than your personality. Its presentation should be practical, with language and style that is as direct as possible. Some standards manuals today are gimmicky productions—design projects rather than reference books. This is a mistake. Since the subject matter of a full-blown graphic standards manual is likely to be very complex, too much design can get in the way of explaining and showing things clearly and may actually hinder proper implementation.

Loose-leaf manuals have certain advantages, especially in implementing large programs. They allow more important applications to be developed, disseminated and collected while other solutions are still in the works. Their contents can be split apart, so that various departments receive only the sections they need. If new or modified applications appear in the future, binders can be easily updated.

The typical manual is arranged by broad subject categories. After the management message, you should present and describe the new logomark and state how it should and should not be used. If there is a corporate color or colors, give samples with the appropriate color-matching numbers and typical uses. Then present the graphic details of the company's organizational hierarchy and naming system, along with details about permitted typefaces, divisional name placement, and any recommended colors beyond the corporate color.

These basic exhibits set the stage for the myriad applications to follow: corporate and divisional business papers and cards, publications, signage, vehicles, et al. At the end of the manual, provide black-and-white repro materials and color chips. The former keep people from using third- and fourth-generation materials for repro; the latter keep them from guessing which shade is the right one.

In developing the graphic standards manual for Mary Kay Cosmetics, Sibley/Peteet first prepared tightly sketched comps for client approval. They then created the final product. This is the manual cover.

Typical divider spread.

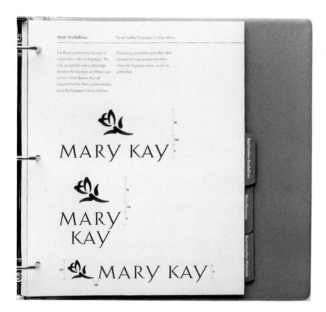

Floral symbol and logotype.

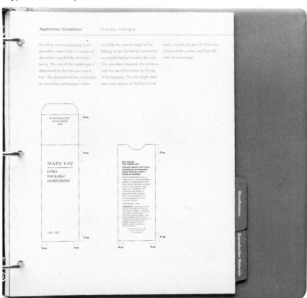

Secondary packaging guidelines.

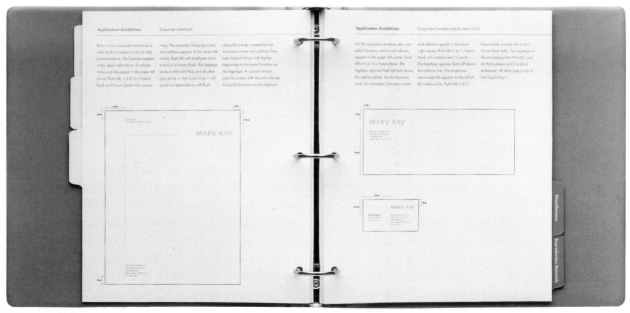

Stationery guidelines.

In setting up application examples, try to anticipate how the guidelines will be used and what questions the users might have. Is it permissible to use the symbol without the logotype? When? What rules govern the situation? Which officers, departments and operations get their own letterheads? How will their names appear? Can the sales department print its own letterhead for a special promotion? What are the rules? What if someone needs something that's not illustrated in the manual? What are the channels for staying within the system? Anticipating user needs up front can keep the identity from being compromised later on.

How many and which applications your manual should include is a function of need, budget, the complexity of the program, and how loosely (or tightly) the identity system has been conceived. A company that hires out work to many designers or that has no design manager will need bullet-proof specifications for everything; a business with a single, long-standing relationship with a designer, especially if that person is the identity designer, can succeed with fewer. Here is a list of core elements that a typical large corporate identity manual might contain:

• An introduction to the corporate identity program — table of contents, CEO's message, instructions for using the manual, glossary of corporate identity terms.

• The new graphic identity — basic logomark; permitted logotype/symbol variations; consistent use of logomark with do's and don'ts; logomark as corporate signature and as used with divisional signatures; typographic standards for use with logomark, including font manufacturer.

• Business papers — general considerations such as location of logomark, color, typography, paper stocks, followed by specific applications.

• Corporate publications, such as annual reports and newsletters, if applicable — general guidelines (placement of corporate signature; grids and layouts; column widths and line spacings; picture placement; type specs, including font manufacturer) followed by specific applications.

• Advertising and sales materials — general guidelines (placement of corporate signature, grids and layouts for different sizes) followed by specific applications.

• Architectural/environmental signage, if applicable — general guidelines (environmental positioning, local vs. long-distance; colors and materials) followed by specific applications.

• Vehicular signage, if applicable — general guidelines (placement, colors, paint vs. decals) followed by specific applications.

• Products and services materials, such as warranty materials, if applicable — general guidelines followed by specific applications.

• Packaging, including shipping materials or gift cartons, if applicable — general guidelines followed by specific applications.

• Clothing, such as uniforms, if applicable — general guidelines followed by specific applications.

• Other applications.

The actual contents of each section will vary according to your client's needs. Items that may apply to your client are listed at the end of this chapter by category of client. (See pages 72-73.)

Small Company Guidelines. Most designers find that the lion's share of their identity jobs are for small businesses, where the owner is both client and identity manager. Graphics programs for these companies may be simply a logomark and stationery system, or they may include a few dozen applications. Because implementation is limited, and because it isn't likely that the client will have a lot of designers producing communications at many locations, small businesses usually don't need full-blown graphic standards manuals.

But your client's new identity system will have a better chance of success if you provide some sort of guidelines. What form these take will vary with the client's specific circumstances. A woodcrafter with a basic stationery package, for example, may need only a typewritten user's guide, reordering information, and perhaps a few prints of the logomark to apply to ads or fliers. On the other hand, a small manufacturing firm with one hundred employees may need business pa-

November 1986

Greg Boattenhamer
Director of Communications
Iowa Hospital Association
100 East Grand
Des Moines, Iowa 50309

Dear Greg:

I am pleased to enclose the Graphic Standards Manual for the
National Institute for Rural Health Policy. This information
is a guide for all persons who prepare printed and visual
communications for the institute.

Because the logo — and indeed the organization itself — is new,
you may wish to consult with us regarding various usages of your
trademark. Please feel free to call on us for any information
which is not included here or which is unclear.

Best wishes for the continued success of the National Institute
for Rural Health Policy.

Sincerely,

Sheree L. Clark
Account Supervisor

SAYLES GRAPHIC DESIGN, INC.
304½ 8th Street
Suite 216
Des Moines, Iowa
50309

National Institute

for Rural

Health Policy

100 East Grand

Des Moines, Iowa

50309

(515) 288-1955

Corporate Identification Program

GRAPHIC STANDARDS GUIDELINES

This information is a guide for all persons who prepare printed
and visual communications for the National Institute for Rural
Health Policy.

Co-sponsored by the Iowa
Hospital Education and
Research Foundation and
the University of Iowa
Center for Health Services
Research

Introduction:

Graphic standards are developed to insure consistent usage of a
corporate identity program. These guidelines will help you
prepare your communications in accordance with standards in use
at this time.

The Logo:

The logo of the National Institute for Rural Health Policy is a
tire-shaped, circular object. On institute stationery it is
printed in black hot leaf; in newsprint or on paper stock where
hot leaf is impractical, the logo will appear as 100% black.
When used in one-color publications when the color used is not
black, the logo is to appear as 100% of the color being utilized.

The Logo Background:

The "background" for the institute logo — which should be used
whenever possible — is representative of earth or soil. On
institute stationery the background soil is PMS 401 (100%). When
used in newsprint or where PMS reproduction is impossible, a screen
of approximately 10%-20% should be used. The screen should not be
so dark as to obliterate any type appearing over it. The
institute logo (the tire-shaped object) is to rest upon the
background soil.

Typography:

"The National Institute for Rural Health Policy" should appear in
Helvetica Medium. The words "co-sponsored by the Iowa Hospital
Education and Research Foundation and the University of Iowa
Center for Health Services Research" should appear in Helvetica
light. On institute stationery all typography is 100% black.

Logo Placement:

The logo may be used in different positions on a printed page.
On stationery the logo is always in the upper left of the
letterhead and envelope.

Stationery Reordering Information:

The first order for national Institute for Rural Health Policy
stationery was placed in October 1986. 5000 sheets of letterhead
and 5000 envelopes were ordered. 1000 second sheets were also
ordered at that time. Additional supplies, including photostats
of the institute logo may be obtained from Sayles Graphic Design,
Inc. The logo and its usage are the property of the National
Institute for Rural Health Policy.

The first order of stationery was printed on 24# Protocol 100;
the envelopes were produced with 100# Protocol.

The envelopes produced for the institute must be fabricated (also
called "converted") because of the hot leaf treatment of the
logo. This process takes a minimum of two weeks. Please keep
this in mind when reordering.

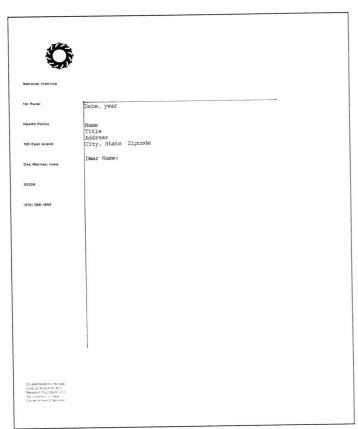

Guidelines prepared by Sayles Graphic Design for the National Institute for Rural Health Policy. This mini-manual opens with a message from the design firm encouraging the client to ask for help in developing further uses of their new identifier. Copy and illustrations describe program elements, give instructions for reordering stationery, and provide typing guidelines for business papers. The whole package was slipped inside an inexpensive plastic report cover for presentation to the client.

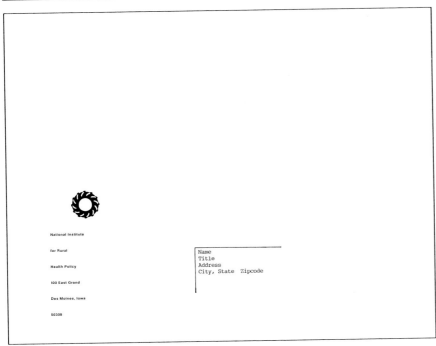

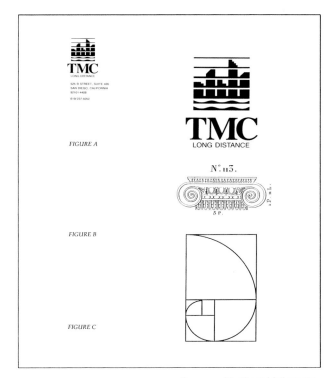

FIGURE A

FIGURE B

FIGURE C

Two-page identity guidelines prepared by Bennett Peji for TMC Long Distance explain the basics and also supply a feel for their interpretation in other applications.

pers and forms, as well as signage, advertising and promotional guidelines.

Such guidelines don't have to be an expensive production. You can type and slip into a plastic cover the basic information about the logomark and its proper use, color, placement, and important spatial relationships to be maintained. Include as needed other pertinent contents — for example, sample printed stationery and reordering information, repro materials, and/or precise specifications for items such as invoices and business cards that will be reordered frequently. (Check the lists on pages 72-73 to see what considerations might apply.) The important thing is to provide users with enough information to safeguard your client's identity investment.

Client Approval. As each group of applications is developed, show them to the client or working committee for input and approval or modification. You may use interim, or temporary, guidelines as a means of putting the guidelines in the field, working out the bugs, and reaching final approval. Or you can develop and assemble applications into a rough manual, where they and their documentation receive simultaneous approval.

For smaller companies with only a few applications, you can present comps for a complete system all at once. These materials may well be finalized, "real-world" versions of the examples you showed at the meeting when you first presented the identity design; or they might include some additional applications, as well. The difference will be that these final layouts will be camera-ready art, with live type and production methods carefully thought out. Once the identity has been standardized for all applications, you are ready to tackle full-scale implementation.

The Launch

Since the complete implementation of a graphic identity system can be a lengthy and time-consuming process, it's important to get it off to a good start. Both large and small businesses can do this by staging an identity launch — an official event introducing the new graphic identity system.

An official identity launch is a good way to heighten awareness that some important changes are taking place within a company, and to motivate employees at all levels in support of the new identity. It explains the company and its business, where it is going, and how the new identity will help get it there. Although some of the new identity materials may already be in place at the time of the official launch, the event is still important because it puts the implementation process into an official context. This is the time to persuade any holdouts that the new graphic identity needs their commitment and support. Your client will want to make the most of this opportunity to address key influential audiences (shareholders, employees, the financial community) about the changes taking place within the company.

The launch event itself can take many forms. It can be an official memorandum sent to all employees, or an audiovisual presentation shown to managers and sales staffs. It could be a printed brochure explaining the identity basics, or a special issue of the company newsletter devoted to complete coverage of the topic. It could make a splash with advertisements in local newspapers and the financial press. Or it might combine these elements with other tactics—a stage show, a press conference, a company-wide "Identity Day."

The timing of the launch is important. It should come when the identity program is ready for full implementation and manuals or guidelines are ready to be put into the hands of users. You will have worked out with the client a schedule for the implementation process that reflects client priorities as well as production considerations. Some clients will want to change their identity overnight, especially if the legal status or name of the company has been changed. With an "overnight" identity change, the new identity is announced, and, on the energy created by that event, is quickly and forcefully implemented across the company. This method avoids confusion over just who the company is and how it looks. However, this is also the most expensive route, as anything bearing the old graphic identifiers must be immediately thrown out and re-

placed. If your client is not willing to bear the cost (and the waste), gradual implementation is the way to go.

Gradual implementation works especially well when the identity change is an evolutionary one. New corporate materials should be printed before the launch and put in use right away. All advertising and other communications reaching large audiences would, of course, also need to reflect the change immediately. But other materials can be phased in as need dictates and current stocks are depleted. On the negative side, a gradual implementation means that, for a time, both the old and the new identities will exist side by side. This may cause some confusion among employees and in the marketplace.

After the official launch, implementation continues across the company until its entire face has been changed. It is up to the identity designer to keep the ball rolling and, if necessary, remedy any flagging enthusiasm as time goes on. Implementation can be a long and arduous process, but when done with vigilance, it results in a lasting and effective corporate identity.

Identity Applications

The following checklists reflect possible applications for different types of identity programs, organized by categories of clients; materials that might be used by a broad spectrum of clients are listed as "Common Applications." Most work you do for nonprofit organizations will probably require the applications listed under "Common Applications." Large nonprofits, such as hospitals and colleges or other educational institutions, will probably need applications more like those suggested for large corporations. (See the Case Study for Buena Vista College, pages 88-95, for an example of the different applications such an institution may have.) Your discussion of each application in the manual or guidelines should include copy that describes and explains the solution, including what is and isn't flexible, and also give exact specifications (measurements for margins, placement on the page, type sizes, paper names and weights, etc.) for reproducing it.

Corporate Identity Applications

Common Applications

- Letterheads for corporate and divisional offices.
  - Executive and standard letterheads.
  - Continuing (or second) sheets.
  - Memos.
  - Press releases.
  - Executive and standard business cards.
  - Envelopes (no. 10 and others).
  - Mailing labels.
- Forms (billheads, purchase orders, shipping forms, etc.; computerized and standard; horizontal and vertical formats).
  - Ads for products/services.
  - Direct mail.
  - Posters and brochures.
  - Exterior and/or interior sign system(s).
  - Annual (or quarterly) report.
  - Newsletter.

Large Corporations

- Items listed under "common applications."
- Items listed under the appropriate client category.
  - Recruiting/training literature.
  - Human resources documents.
  - Regional and divisional ads.
  - Recruitment ads.
  - Exhibition materials.
  - Exterior and interior sign systems.
  - Directional signs.
  - Corporate flag.
  - Employee identification materials.
  - Nameplates.
  - Parking lot stickers.

Companies that Manufacture a Product

- Items listed under "common applications."
- Items listed under the appropriate client category.
  - Recruiting/training literature.
  - Human resources documents.
  - Corporate and/or divisional ads.
  - Product ads.
  - Catalogs.
  - Merchandisers.
  - Exhibition materials.
  - Promotional items.
  - External service vehicles (trucks, vans, autos, freighters, tankers, airplanes, railway cars, etc.).
  - Internal vehicles (forklifts, etc.).
  - Product design and identification.
  - Warranty materials.
  - Operating instructions.
  - Delivery/installation instructions.
  - Product packaging.
  - Product wrappers/labels.
  - Gift cartons.
  - Plastic and paper bags.
  - Tubes.
  - Shippers/labels.
  - Uniforms.
  - Coveralls.
  - Lab coats/smocks (if applicable).
  - Employee identification materials.
  - Safety hats.

Clothing-Related Businesses

- Items listed under "common applications."
  - Catalogs.
  - Merchandisers (counter displays, etc.).
  - Promotional items (stickers, pennants, ties/scarves).
  - Delivery vehicles (if applicable).
  - In-house/retail display systems.
  - Hangtags.
  - Garment bags.
  - Shopping bags, regular bags.
  - Gift tags.
  - Gift certificates.

- Product packaging.
- Product wrappers/labels.
- Gift cartons.
- Shippers/labels.
- Employee uniforms, smocks or name pins.
- Employee identification materials.
- Training materials.

Service Businesses
- Items listed under "common applications."
- Promotional items (stickers, pennants, ties/scarves, lapel pins and other giveaways).
- Delivery vehicles (if applicable).
- Employee uniforms, smocks or name pins.
- Employee identification materials.
- Training materials.
- Client-specific materials (special envelopes for photographs for a film processor, for example).
- Exhibition materials.
- Capabilities package or brochure.

Restaurants
- Items listed under "common applications."
- Menus.
- Tableware (cups, glasses, plates, napkins).
- Matchbooks.
- Employee uniforms, smocks or name pins.
- Employee identification materials.
- Training materials.
- Promotional items.
- Take-out containers.

Retail (Not Clothing-Related)
- Items listed under "common applications."
- Catalogs.
- Merchandisers (counter displays, etc.).
- Promotional items (stickers, pennants, ties/scarves, bookmarks, other giveaways).

- Delivery vehicles (if applicable).
- Internal vehicles (forklifts, etc.).
- In-house/retail display systems.
- Gift certificates.
- Gift tags.
- Shopping bags, regular bags.
- Product packaging.
- Product wrappers/labels.
- Gift cartons.
- Shippers/labels.
- Employee uniforms, smocks or name pins.
- Employee identification materials.
- Training materials.
- Special packaging for "house" products.

Lodgings and Real Estate-Related Businesses
- Items listed under "common applications".
- Interior and exterior signage.
- Directional signs.
- Flags or banners.
- Uniforms, smocks or name tags.
- Vehicles (if applicable).
- Employee identification materials.
- Training literature.
- Promotional items (stickers, ties, scarves, food items and other giveaways).
- Regional or national ads.
- Items listed under "retail (not clothing-related)".
- Items listed under "clothing-related businesses" if applicable.
- Items listed under "restaurants," if applicable.
- Parking passes or parking stickers.
- Comment cards.
- Room keys.
- Guest register.
- Linens.
- Notepaper and stationery for guests.
- Amenities (for lodgings).

Case Studies

··

Corporate identity programs for smaller businesses and institutions can be both challenging and rewarding. Each of the seven programs examined here was developed to its own unique criteria, within a particular working method, and in expression of a distinctive corporate personality.

Northwest Passage, an organization to promote travel and tourism (Larson Design Associates), pages 76-83.

The Together Center, a learning and recreational facility for young teens (River City Studio), pages 84-87.

Buena Vista College, a small, private college (Sayles Graphic Design), pages 88-95.

Bayside-To-Go, a shop offering mementos bearing the name of the retail complex, Bayside Marketplace, in which it is located (Sullivan Perkins), pages 96-99.

Sleeman Brewing and Malting Company, a Canadian brewery (Taylor & Browning Design Associates), pages 100-103.

Souper Salad, a restaurant chain and catering business (Midnight Oil Studios), pages 104-109.

Post-Industrial Stress & Design, a multi-product company encompassing a commercial printer doing business as Post-Industrial Press, a T-shirt and greeting card operation, and an operation producing fine art serigraphs (Art Chantry Design), pages 110-115.

Northwest Passage

Larson Design Associates, of Rockford, Illinois, has long been design consultant to the Rockford Area Convention and Visitors Bureau. Working with the bureau's executive director, Wendy Fisher, Jeff Larson and his staff have through the years produced a number of successful and highly visible promotions to lure business people and tourists to the Rockford area.

In 1989, the Illinois government created a statewide economic development program that would capitalize on each region's distinctive attributes. Dubbed "Corridors of Opportunity" and administered by the state's Department of Commerce and Community Affairs (DCCA), the program worked at the grass-roots level through a committee of DCCA-appointed delegates from each county within the various development corridors. The Northwest Corridor committee, representing the seven counties along Illinois' northwestern borders with Wisconsin and Iowa, was composed of twenty citizens representing a range of interests such as farmers, small business operators, homemakers — and a few professionals with expertise at promoting the local economy. One of these was Wendy Fisher.

The committee's basic task was to decide how to market its corridor, what was to be promoted and how, and who would be hired to do it. In the discussion process, Fisher, Kathleen Webster and Connie Zorn (her counterparts in Jo Daviess and Stephenson counties) emerged as strong voices in determining the area's selling points.

One of the first things the committee did was hire two Rockford-area advertising and marketing communications experts, Jay Graham, of Graham/Spencer Advertising, and Jack Cratty, of Cratty & Associates. Graham and Cratty helped guide the twenty committee members through the early and sometimes heated discussions. The key was developing a plan that would express the common attractions of the Northwest Corridor, while at the same time finding for each county a unique selling point.

With the ground prepared and a marketing plan roughed out, the committee turned its attention to the Northwest Corridor's graphic image and marketing communications. Several area design firms were invited to make presentations, among them Larson Design Associates.

Before meeting with the committee, Larson did his homework. The committee provided him a budget for the first year and expressed the need for an identity and some basic promotional materials, such as ads, brochures and posters. In addition, Larson met with Cratty and Graham to gather background information and to work out areas of responsibility.

Larson's initial presentation included no preliminary designs or other sketches. "I'm a strong believer in not doing spec work," Larson says. "I think designers who do only hurt themselves. They won't have done the groundwork yet, and so their presentation will have to be off target."

Instead, Larson showed his studio's portfolio and described how job responsibilities would be shared among the three consultants involved — that is, that all three would be involved in laying the groundwork, and that Larson Design would be responsible for producing the graphic identity and all the printed material. Although Larson had been asked for a one-year proposal, he also described what might be accomplished in a second year, should the project be extended.

The committee was impressed with Larson's grasp of its needs and with his comprehensive research and planning. Within a few days, the designer was informed that he had the job. Numerous meetings followed — with the entire committee and with Wendy Fisher, Connie Zorn, and Kathleen Webster — to try to bring into agreement the members' many needs and voices. At last, after months of discussion, the design and marketing team was ready to begin the quest for identity.

Since the Northwest Corridor's graphic identity would determine the look of all the printed materials, developing a mark was the consultants' first priority. To become more familiar with the corridor, Larson, Graham and Cratty spent a weekend traveling through it, much as would the tourists they hoped to bring into the area. Armed with a list of attractions, they stayed at bed-and-breakfasts, visited camp-grounds and duck farms, and ate pie and drank coffee in roadside cafes. They talked with local shop-keepers, folks they met in diners, and duck hunters coming off the river. They climbed atop a river-boat abandoned along the Missis-sippi, and hired a small plane to better view the rolling countryside. Everywhere they went, they took photographs.

On the drive back to Rockford, Larson and his cohorts discussed what they had seen and felt during their three-day tour. Someone spoke what was to become the pro-gram's catchphrase—"the rug-ged, beautiful hills of northwestern Illinois"—and Larson began sketch-ing some ideas. "I felt the identity needed to be a logo," Larson says, "but it also needed to be more. It needed to convey a feel for the whole area."

1. Scratchboard landscape: "Too obvious."

2. Scratchboard landscape with border (idea later adapted to a poster).

3. River with border: "Too illustrative, but river theme good."

4. Simplified landscape with type trial.

5. Landscape reversed: "Creates more mass."

6. Landscape copied onto Speckletone: "Rugged, rough landscape, but need to create a 'passage.' Mood good."

7. Simplified river passage. Back in the office the next morning, Larson resumed his exploratory sketches. Within a few days, with the transparencies from the excursion in hand, he pushed those ideas further. "The roughs just started simplifying themselves," he says about the process, "into what became a passage—a passage to somewhere rugged, somewhere away from it all." When he felt he had found a direction, he used a photocopier to reduce and enlarge his sketches and developed a roughened texture. Finally, as a reality check, he put one of these copies on a sheet of Speckletone, the paper he was considering for the letterhead stock. The feel was right. All that remained was to define the river passage.

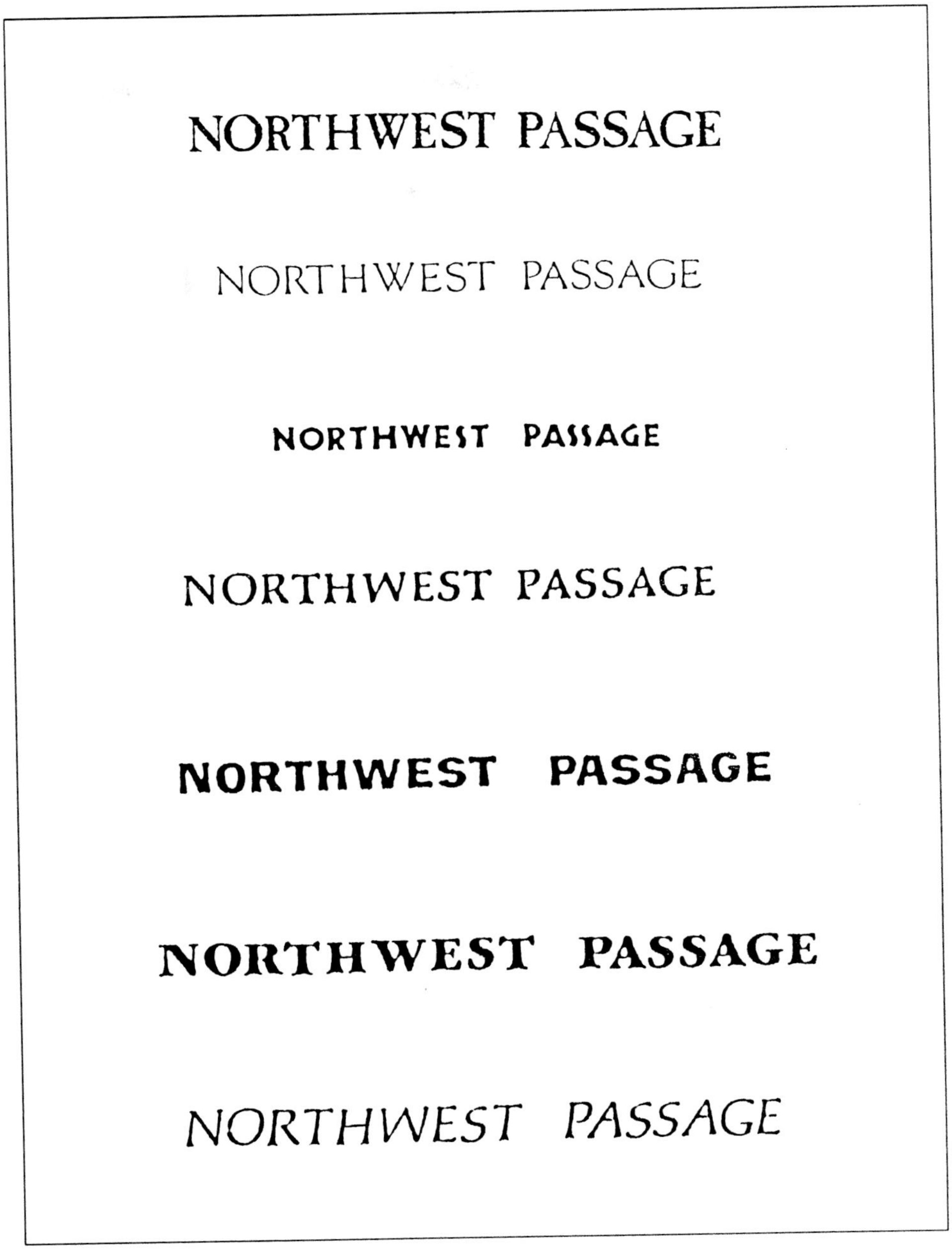

NORTHWEST PASSAGE

NORTHWEST PASSAGE

NORTHWEST PASSAGE

NORTHWEST PASSAGE

NORTHWEST PASSAGE

NORTHWEST PASSAGE

NORTHWEST PASSAGE

NORTH
WEST
PASSAGE

With the river image and the Speckletone's tactile attributes in mind, Larson looked for a suitable typeface. He quickly came to Caslon Antique (bottom), a traditional face with "a refined yet rugged appeal." Larson showed his colleagues the visual record of his development process. Together they discussed various modes of execution, and his colleagues gave his ideas ample support. Next, Larson set up a meeting with the Northwest Corridor committee.

Because the identifier in its finished form would have a rough texture — to capture the down-home, rugged look the consultants had agreed upon — Larson took the mark to final art before the client presentation so the committee would actually see that texture. The most significant changes were the logotype's second-line addition of a compass pointing northwest, and the selection of a warm, rich orange as the "company" color.

To give the committee an idea of how the mark would work, the identity was presented in its environment. Larson had colored transfers made of the proposed logomark and comped it into a letterhead (left), a poster (facing page, bottom right), and a brochure aimed at group tours (shown both front and back on the facing page, immediate right). It was this last comp that sold the committee on the idea, the designer says.

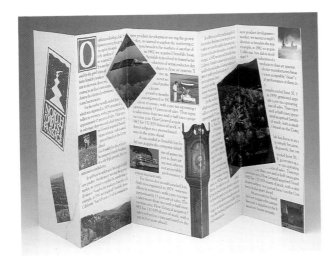

Photo reference for the poster. (The photo was also used in a brochure.)

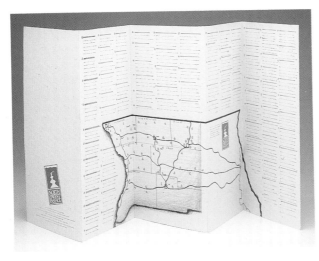

"Only one idea, one design was presented," Larson says. "I've found that if you give a committee too many choices to make a decision, the last thing you'll get is a decision."

Larson's proposed design received full committee consent. The only discussion involved details as to exactly what would be shown in the brochure. "But the overall presentation went without a hitch." Finally, the comps were submitted to the state Department of Commerce and Community Affairs, where they also received full approval.

This poster was adapted from the photo shown above it, and from a rejected logomark study, shown on page 78.

Larson went on to produce final art for the letterhead, a news release and a tour brochure. For the poster, he asked Chicago illustrator Cheryl Winser to hand-color a mezzotint of one of the excursion photographs, which was also used in the brochure. He co-wrote advertising and brochure copy with Jay Graham. The entire program proved so successful that Larson's proposed second-year extension was also adopted. Since then, Larson Design Associates has remained the designer for the Northwest Passage Corridor Council.

Wed like to share a secret to warm your traveler's heart. It's about thoughtfully preserved memories and stunning natural landscapes. It's about entertainment sparkling on stages and delicious food steaming on table tops. It's about endless outdoor recreational settings, from green fairways to green-canopied hiking trails. And it's about *convenience*, because treasures like these and more, are waiting in seven counties of rugged, beautiful hills in the nearby Northwest Passage of northern Illinois.

In Cooperation with the Department of Commerce and Community Affairs Corridors of Opportunity Program.

Northwest Passage Corridor Council

Carroll, Jo Daviess, Lee, Ogle, Stephenson, Whiteside and Winnebago Counties.

12.5M 6-90 GL

The success of Larson Design's identity and communications program for the council was documented in 1990 through an advertising and direct mail assessment. A series of ads were placed in local newspapers and regional magazines. Those ads brought 9,884 responses, of which a random 1,500 received a mailed questionnaire. The survey found that:

- 74 percent of respondents had visited the area in 1990;
- 51 percent spent the night, 21 percent were on day trips;
- 66 percent of the overnighters stayed in hotels, 18 percent camped;
- 70 percent traveled during the summer (June through August);
- Visits to historic sites increased by 50 percent.

Lee If you'd like to see a Whitehouse that's untarnished by government scandals, huge deficits and political rhetoric, jump in the car and visit Ronald Reagan's Boyhood Home in nearby Dixon, Illinois. It's a trip back into the time of iceboxes and radio, when every boy had a pennant on his wall and a frog in his pocket. Lowell Park is nearby, also in Dixon, where lifeguard "Dutch" Reagan is said to have pulled 77 drowning swimmers from

the rolling waters of the Rock River. If it's railroad history you're interested in, head for the little town of Amboy and the Amboy Depot Museum. Housed in an old railway depot, you'll not only see a seemingly endless variety of artifacts and photographs, you'll touch them and smell them, too...this museum is just a little musty, and proud of it! In fact, spending time here is like spending time in an old friend's attic (a well organized attic, mind you), full of old secrets, surprises and memories.

People who say you have to drive hundreds of miles to buy great antiques are off their rockers. They should visit Galena in the nearby Northwest Passage, then they'll really see the light. We're right here, just over your horizon in the rugged, beautiful hills of northern Illinois. Call today for a colorful, free brochure on all the fun and interesting things to do in the Northwest Passage, including the wonders of antiquing in Jo Daviess County and Galena. Dial toll free daily, 800-747-8474.

Northwest Passage Corridor Council · Carroll, Jo Daviess, Lee, Ogle, Stephenson, Whiteside, Winnebago
In Cooperation with the Department of Commerce and Community Affairs Corridors of Opportunity Program.

The Together Center

Designer Deb Turpin is a member of the board of the Together Center, a learning and recreational facility in downtown Kansas City, Missouri. The center targets young teens in the area. Since 1987, Turpin's River City Studio, which she operates with partner Jamie Corning, has been supporting the center with public service design work.

In late 1989, Carol Albright, director of the Together Center, approached Turpin about creating a new logomark and letterhead for the facility. Turpin in turn passed the assignment to staff designer and illustrator David Butler for concept development and design exploration.

The center's existing graphics consisted of a black-and-white letterhead printed on inexpensive stock. There were no cards or envelopes. The existing logotype conveyed neither the purpose of the Together Center nor its sense of commitment and vitality.

After assessing the Together Center audience of teens and their parents, counselors and benefactors, Butler came to the conclusion that the center needed not just a logotype, but a graphic that would be both purposeful and inviting. Images of encircling arms, the center's building, and kids immediately came to mind; Butler sketched them out.

togetHer
center

Together
Center

TOGETHER CENTER

Once Butler had some ideas he liked, he cut them from amberlith. "Amberlith works well for me," Butler says, "because it gives the client a really good feel for how the final art will look. It's also a lot faster than inking or even markering my ideas, and it helps solidify theories in my mind about how they will look as a finished piece."

Butler then took the amberlith roughs to the computer and began brainstorming logotypes on the screen. Because they were cut from amberlith, Butler could place the roughs directly against the screen for one-on-one matching with prospective logotypes.

togetHer
center

"Maybe *too* together. Looks like they have turtle heads. Doesn't relay an inviting feeling or sense of place."

Together
Center

"We like it. But can you fix the fingers?"

TOGETHER CENTER

"Maybe *too* contemporary. Looks like it might be a blood bank. The house here is not as well defined as in the other roughs."

Once he had matched up likely partners, the designer made black-and-white prints of four designs and sent them over to the client for review and comment. Because of the charitable nature of the designer/client relationship and the need to save expensive design time, no personal presentations were made.

After some discussion, the board sent the black-and-white prints back with members' comments. Interestingly, the board accepted one idea right away, with only minor modifications.

Together
Center

"The house looks strange, but this is a good direction. Not crazy about the type."

Together
Center

Butler created a final amberlith cut and the repro logomark.

With the identifier chosen, Butler went on to select card and stationery stock and prepare a marker comp. The proposed paper was a crisp white twenty-pound writing sheet. The identity was expanded into a background graphic that could be printed across each piece in a 10 percent tint of the logomark color. Butler chose a soft yet distinctive color for each item.

The designer sent the comp to the client just as he had the sample logomarks. "Maybe they didn't want to take advantage of our free work," Butler muses, "or maybe they agreed with us as to direction. But they chose without correction all of the elements we presented."

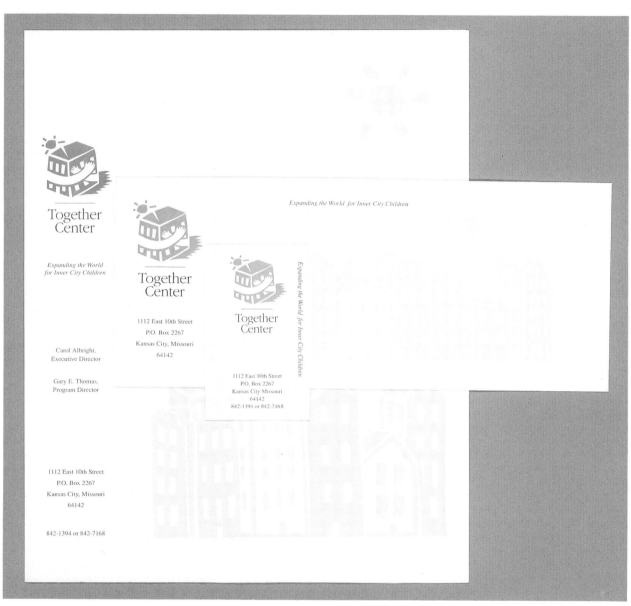

The Together Center's final, printed stationery does all the right things. The new logomark communicates a warm, loving environment, and the production looks responsible and businesslike, without being wasteful. Since none of the stationery items could be printed on the same press at the same time anyway, Butler's choice of individual colors for each piece added only the cost of ink-mixing and washup to the printing bill. And, when the printer heard that both the design and the paper were being contributed free of charge, he tore up his own bill. "The only cost," Butler states, "was the type, which was one disk run out for all the elements — about thirty bucks."

Buena Vista College: Centennial Logomark

Buena Vista (be-you-na vista) is a small, private college with an enrollment of one thousand. It's situated on the shores of Storm Lake in northwestern Iowa. In 1987, Sayles Graphic Design had made a presentation to Susan Cameron, the college's director of public relations, in hope of landing a recruiting account. That job ended up going to someone else, but two years later, when the school was looking for an unusual logo to celebrate its one-hundredth anniversary, Cameron remembered Sayles.

Cameron was in a bind. As she explained to Sayles' managing partner in charge of new accounts, Sheree Clark, Buena Vista (or BV, as the college is familiarly called) had unsuccessfully been trying to develop the logo internally. Now, the school's president was leaving on an overseas sabbatical in one week. Could Sayles Graphic Design get something together on approval before then?

Despite the tight timing, the design firm was eager to work with the college. After consulting with partner/art director John Sayles, Clark set up an appointment for the following Sunday. Before the meeting, Clark and Cameron agreed that, regardless of whether the preliminary design was approved, BV would pay a flat fee for the presentation. If the proposal met with the president's approval, Sayles would receive an agreed-upon sum to take the concept to final art. Clark and Cameron also developed a fee schedule for applying the logo to various stationery materials. All terms were discussed, agreed upon, and formalized in a letter before work began.

Following studio policy of presenting one concept at a time, Sayles set about finding a single centennial logo that would convey a sense of tradition, while at the same time reflecting the centennial theme, "New Vistas."

Sayles' logomark search revolved around a monogrammatic use of Buena Vista's nickname, BV, and a familiar campus landmark, the Victory Arch. Sayles centered an arch shape over the "V," creating a torchlike image at the heart of the monogram.

At the first presentation meeting, Sayles and Clark showed both black-and-white and color versions of the proposed logomark, as well as cut-paper comps of its application to centennial letterheads and collateral. Cameron liked the design and the next day presented it to BV's president, who gave immediate approval.

Comp of Buena Vista centennial stationery. Because paper for the campaign would be specially manufactured, Sayles used Pantone ® papers for the comps. A cut-paper and marker comp of president's special centennial stationery was also created.

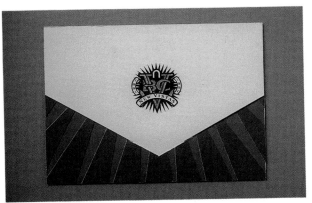

Comp of informal, self-mailing notecards, which could also be used as invitations for centennial events. A similar piece, a comp of a pocket folder to hold centennial materials, was also shown.

Comp of centennial banners.

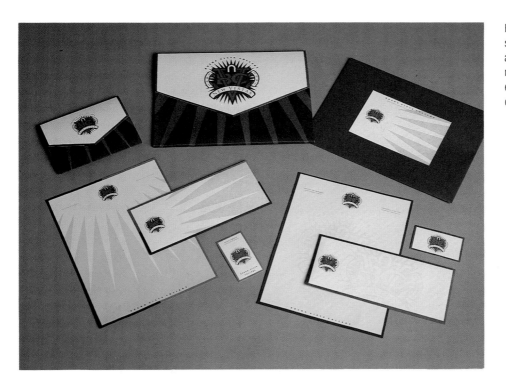

For the final art, Sayles refined the sizing of the monogram initials and arch, and altered the angle of the rays. The final logomark and printed pieces, however, are still very close to his original concept.

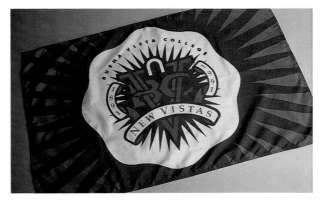

The centennial logo was also applied to flags presented to the town of Storm Lake, the Iowa Historical Society, and others in conjunction with Buena Vista's centennial celebrations; to banners displayed at various college events; and to sportswear and other novelty items for sale in the college bookstore. Designer Sayles served as consultant in the selection of items and specification of colors.

Buena Vista College: Permanent Logomark

At about the same time, the Buena Vista admissions staff was interviewing designers for its recruitment materials. Susan Cameron suggested Sayles Graphic Design make a presentation.

Uncertain just who would be at the interview, Clark and Sayles assembled a slide program of past work and brought along some printed samples, in case the group was small. Since the centennial logomark wasn't public yet, the duo got Cameron's permission to show it at the conclusion of the presentation.

The strategy worked: Sayles Graphic Design was asked to prepare a complete admissions campaign. In addition, Sayles' centennial monogram was so well received by the Buena Vista administration that they asked him to adapt the mark for use beyond 1991 as a permanent logomark. Although Sayles initially offered the logomark design in more subdued colors, ultimately the centennial colors were retained in the permanent mark. It was this mark that became the centerpiece for the recruitment campaign.

Sweatshirts bearing the centennial and permanent Buena Vista monograms.

The final version of the new Buena Vista College permanent logomark (center) was adapted from the centennial logo (top). Also shown is the new athletic mark featuring BV's beaver mascot (bottom).

Buena Vista's existing recruitment materials had a soft look focused on the theme "Imagine." Sayles wanted to develop a stronger image.

Sketches and amber cuts worked out for some of BV's recruiting pieces.

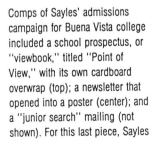

Sayles' original idea (top) for a table-top recruitment mailer targeted to guidance counselors proved too expensive to reproduce. His modified effort (bottom) cut unit cost from $3.86 to about $2.00.

Comps of Sayles' admissions campaign for Buena Vista college included a school prospectus, or "viewbook," titled "Point of View," with its own cardboard overwrap (top); a newsletter that opened into a poster (center); and a "junior search" mailing (not shown). For this last piece, Sayles developed a customized kaleidoscope to carry through the "Point of View" theme; inside is the Buena Vista logomark.

For added drama in the presentation, Sayles had the proposed logomark silkscreened onto a sweatshirt (bottom).

The final admissions campaign, imprinted with the new Buena Vista logomark. The corrugated cardboard "sculpture" sent to high school guidance counselors (left) can stand alone or hang on a wall.

A prospective student's first introduction to BV is the "Point of View" mailing, which invites students to "take a closer look at Buena Vista" through the custom kaleidoscope (below).

The centerpiece of the admissions campaign (facing page, top), the prospectus contains critical admissions information as well as an application form. It speaks in the same voice as other campaign elements.

BV's six-by-nine-inch recruitment newsletter, "Viewpoint," sent to prospective students (facing page, bottom), reflects the strength of Sayles' logomark design. It opens to become a poster.

Besides developing centennial and recruitment materials, the design firm became involved in other, smaller projects, such as a brochure for the BV Conference Center. In addition, the firm began developing a set of standards to govern use of the permanent logomark after its official adoption in 1992. Because of the scope and number of projects involved, Sayles found ways to economize. Different departments doing similar or simultaneous projects shared production costs.

Sayles also suggested that BV purchase paper for use during the entire centennial year for letterheads, admission materials and other communications. The vast quantity of paper required allowed a custom mill order for the college. Since one of the school's colors is gold, Sayles developed a mustard-gold sheet with flocking (small, hairlike fibers) in purple, blue and red—the other colors in the centennial campaign. The paper was expressly manufactured for Buena Vista by the James River Paper Company.

Bayside-To-Go

The Rouse Co., developers of well-known waterside attractions such as Faneuil Hall in Boston and South Street Seaport in New York City, was in the midst of a similar rehab in the heart of Miami, called Bayside Marketplace. They asked Dallas design firm Sullivan Perkins, who had worked with Rouse on other mall projects and was developing support materials for Bayside's grand opening, to devise an identity for a proposed shop that would sell T-shirts, coffee mugs, beach towels, wristwatches and other mementos bearing the Bayside name.

The shop's new owner, Carole Ann Taylor, was an entrepreneur working on a tight budget that did not allow for air travel. Since the physical distance—and the air fare—between Dallas and Miami was prohibitive, Sullivan Perkins pursued the project through telephone, fax, and overnight delivery services.

In their first conversations with Taylor, the designers found out everything they could about how Taylor envisioned the shop—size, layout, location, decor and inventory—and what she wanted to name it. Taylor had already come up with several naming possibilities, including Bay-side Collection and Bayside Company Store. But she wanted the design team to think about names, too.

Since Sullivan Perkins had developed identities for similar stores in other malls, they quickly picked up on Taylor's needs. The naming process was headed up by partner Mark Perkins, who worked with Sullivan Perkins copywriters to develop categories that would serve as guides in name development. These classifications were loose and wide-ranging—from geographic references, to the nature of the shop's merchandise. Then the naming team went away to individually think about names.

The first phase of the naming process yielded a few hundred possibilities, which Perkins personally reduced to a master list of 105 names. Of these, fifty-nine were considered real contenders and were hand-lettered onto individual cards, which were sent to Taylor along with instructions on how to think about the cards. Taylor reviewed the carded names and began eliminating ones she didn't like. From the group that remained, Bayside-To-Go was her first choice.

With the name selected, the designers proceeded to develop the shop's graphic identity.

Here are some of the names considered by the shop's owner, Carole Ann Taylor, before she settled on Bayside-To-Go.

Bayside Unlimited	Bayside Namesake
Baysidabilia	The Namesake Store
Baysidology	Bayside Image
Inside Bayside	Bayside Deja Vu
Bayside Trader	Unforgettably Bayside
Bayside USA	Bayside On My Mind
The Bayside Market	Keepsakes
Bayside Gallery	Bayside Carry Out
Bayside Plus	Bayside Sampler
Bayside Supply	Bayside Medley
Baystore	The Bayside Assortment
The Bayside Beach Club	Absolutely Bayside
Baytique	Bayside Companion
Bayside Shop	Positively Bayside
Exclusively Bayside	The City of Bayside
Bayside Exclusives	Bayscelleny
Bayside Express	Miscellaneous Bayside
Essentially Bayside	Along the Bay
Nothing But Bayside	Marketplace Memories
Bayside by Design	Bay Designs

Following their usual procedures, partners Ron Sullivan and Mark Perkins asked various staff designers to work up their ideas for a Bayside-To-Go logomark. These were sent to the client for feedback. Shown are cut paper and pencil ideas submitted by Jon Flaming (top) and Linda Helton (bottom).

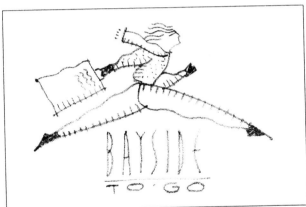

BAYSIDE
MARKETPLACE

Taylor liked the playfulness of Flaming's happy-shopper figure, but his design, she felt, was too far removed from the official Bayside Marketplace logomark (top), which was designed by Communication Arts in Boulder, Colorado. Flaming's final sketch (right) combined the official logotype and a new version of his caricature into a stronger layout, similar to one of Helton's designs.

At this point, Flaming also prepared color roughs, indicating reproduction in flat colors. In the end, however, the designers printed the job four-color process to allow more color flexibility.

Flaming's happy-shopper logo-mark was applied to stationery and business cards, as well as to stickers in three sizes. The stickers were then applied to standard shopping bags, thus saving money that otherwise would have been spent on custom bag conversion. The logomark was also applied to items such as T-shirts, to be sold inside the shop.

Sleeman Brewing and Malting Company

When John Sleeman and his wife, Joanne, opened a pub in Oakville, Ontario, Canada, they were unaware of his family's past involvement in the beer business. It wasn't until he and two partners opened a beer importing firm that an aunt told the entrepreneur about the original Sleeman Brewing and Malting Company, founded by his great-grandfather in 1834. Sleeman resolved to re-establish the family business, which had been out of operation since Prohibition.

By 1987, Sleeman had begun producing beer and ale according to founder George Sleeman's original recipes. He set up his new brewery in Guelph, Ontario—the very town where his great-grandfather had been mayor when he built his original brewery. Sleeman intended his new brews to compete against a dozen or so large and small Canadian breweries for the affluent young adult market. It would have to take on small labels, such as the Upper Canada Brewing Company, as well as giants like Molson and Labatt's. Moreover, Sleeman had little capital for advertising, and would have to rely primarily on packaging to succeed against the competition. When asked to recommend a designer, a mutual friend suggested he call Paul Browning at Toronto's Taylor & Browning Design Associates.

At their first meetings, Sleeman told Browning that he wanted cases and bottles that would emphasize the historical aspects of his company and so help his product stand out against the competition. To help Browning in his visual thinking, he gave the designer some archival materials from the original brewery, including old bottles, labels and wooden cases.

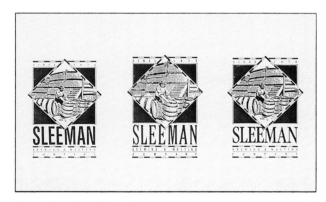

Browning's review of materials from the original brewery inspired these roughs, which he presented to the client for feedback. Both men preferred the circular designs, which suggested a seal of quality.

Browning worked up the seal in bright colors, chosen to appeal to the targeted younger market.

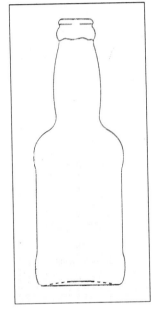

Browning next sketched out a new embossed bottle. The design was dated to the brewery's founding and reinterpreted Sleeman's historical beaver-and-maple-leaf bottle designs. Sleeman thought the embossed beaver and maple leaf — long-standing symbols of Canada — might look good on the seal, too. Browning agreed.

Browning's packaging comps show the beaver and maple leaf replacing the hops-and-grain motif of earlier sketches. At this stage, he suggested red to indicate the brewery's lager products; green, the ale. These color codes were reversed when the design was taken to the final.

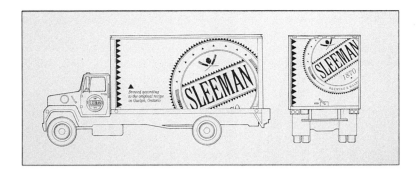

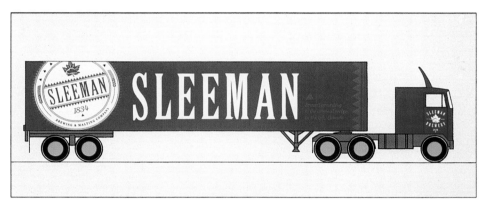

Drawing and comp trials showing the identity applied to delivery transport, and its actual implementation.

Signage at Sleeman's brewery draws on elements applied to packaging and stationery.

Identity is engraved in two colors and gold foil on company stationery (shown above).

The complete Sleeman packaging program (left). Clear glass bottles suggest the purity of the product, and their old-fashioned embossing gives them a "collectible" look. Labels, cartons and other program applications make varying use of the quality seal motif. "In theory," Browning says, "the timeless identities are the ones that have kind of interchangeable characters—not just a straight, one-off symbol, used the same size everywhere. That's why [this program] has various components that can be pulled out and used by themselves. Their collective image overall has more character than the sort of corporate identity where everything is in the top left-hand corner."

Souper Salad

A family-owned restaurant chain, Souper Salad had been serving healthy food in the Boston area for fourteen years. Buoyed by their success, the Reinstein family was contemplating opening a chain of new take-out eateries. But first, they wanted to clean up their company's graphic identity. Their consulting architect suggested they call Midnight Oil Studios, a design and illustration house based in Boston, with a branch office in New York.

Designers James Skiles and Kathryn Klein, the owners of Midnight Oil, met with two of the Reinsteins, Larry and Bruce, to discuss the company's needs and plans for the future. The broth-ers explained their expansion strategy and said they basically wanted Souper Salad's existing graphic identity updated. At the same time, they wanted the designers to suggest the feeling of healthful food. The new identity would eventually be applied to the new take-out restaurant business, as well as to trucks making deliveries to the various Souper Salad locations.

As this was the Reinstein's first experience dealing with a professional graphic design studio (their previous design work had been done by an ad agency), the brothers didn't know quite what to expect. But they did know that they needed help, and that they wanted to keep costs as low as possible.

Souper Salad's existing "soup la-dle" identity, as it appeared on restaurant menus. The Reinstein family asked Midnight Oil Studios for a simple update.

To keep costs as low as possible, designer Skiles showed his clients no sketches, but simply presented a cleaned-up typographic treat-ment. The client loved the concept, and it was immediately applied to a press release, alone, and to a corporate folder, with an added "tossed salad" graphic. At this point, green was used on corporate materials to suggest freshness.

The new take-out restaurants were fast becoming a reality. Aimed at making the fresh and healthy lunch even more accessible to business people, the new restaurants were to be called "Souper Salad Express"—a name that tied in all of the equity of the family's existing operations and also suggested their quick, take-out nature.

Midnight Oil was asked to simply add a script rendition of the word "express" to the new corporate logomark. The designers did that, bypassing the sketch process and directly working up marker comps (above). These achieved a variety of choices through the use of acetate overlays.

However, Klein and Skiles felt that their clients' idea—as good as it was—was not the most exciting solution to the problem. So they submitted another set of ideas as well—the Souper Salad Express Train (left). The clients were delighted, and selected one version for further exploration.

The final Souper Salad Express Train, as applied to paper bags, napkins, sandwich wraps, catering materials and restaurant decor. The take-out bags and packaging functioned as walking billboards and have proved to be terrific advertising vehicles for the new chain.

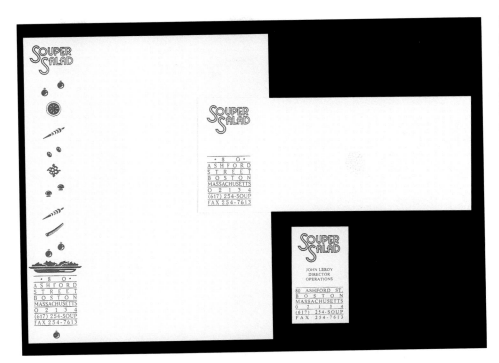

Reversing the usual order of implementation, the new Souper Salad logomark was applied to new corporate stationery (top) only after the more urgent Souper Salad Express applications were finalized. Previous stationery (bottom) had sent a confused and chaotic message.

Finally, the new look was brought home to the original Souper Salad restaurants—full-service eateries featuring fabulous fresh salad bars. Midnight Oil's assignment here was to design menu blanks that could be frequently updated and slipped into plastic menu sleeves.

Because the clients liked the corporate folder cover (see page 104) and wanted to save money, they asked the designers to submit cover designs using the corporate folder idea, in the Express restaurant color scheme. Midnight Oil comped up three cover options (two are shown to the left) and also developed a selection of insert page designs (below).

SOUPER SALAD SALAD BAR

Voted Best by *The Boston Globe*	5.29
All you can eat, but please no sharing.	
Salad Bar & Homemade Soup Combination	6.29
Salad Bar combined with any feature, grilled specialty, sandwich or burger for an additional	3.29

SANDWICHES

Turkey, Havarti & Honey Mustard served on six grain bread.	4.99
Fresh Tarragon Chicken Salad	4.29
Malibu Turkey breast, avocado slices & crisp bacon strips served on herb bread.	5.49
Roast Beef	4.59
Breast of Turkey	4.29
White Albacore Tuna Salad	4.29
Cajun Blackened Chicken Sandwich	5.49
Pan blackened and served with Cajun mayonnaise on six grain bread.	

The above sandwiches are served on six grain, herb, oat bran, our special roll, Syrian pouch or baguette.

BURGERS

The All American	4.59
A full half pound of fresh ground beef, served on our special roll with french fries.	
The Bacon Cheddar	4.99
The same as above, but this one comes topped with cheddar cheese & bacon strips.	

Seasoned Fries	Beer-Battered Onion Rings
2.50	3.99

GRILLED SPECIALTIES

Chinese Barbecued Chicken	6.99
Boneless breast of chicken marinated in our special Oriental barbecue sauce, and then grilled.	
Japanese Grilled Steak	6.99
Marinated beef grilled over charcoal and sliced thin.	
Fresh Herb Sausage	5.99
Fresh ground sausage prepared to perfection over charcoal.	
Souper Salad Combo	6.99
½ order each of Chinese barbecued chicken and fresh herb sausage. "Experience the best of both worlds."	

All grilled specialties served with fresh vegetables

THE SOUPER SALAD FRESH FOOD FEAST

All you can eat of our home-made soup, unlimited Salad Bar & frozen yogurt.	6.99

FEATURES

Texas Melt	5.29
Grilled smoked chicken, cole slaw and smoked ham, covered with tomato slices and melted Havarti cheese. Served open-faced.	
Whole Wheat Vegetable Burrito	5.99
Topped with cheddar cheese, chopped tomatoes, avocados & sour cream.	
Oriental Chicken	5.29
Stir-fry chicken and vegetables served in a pocket.	
Quiche of the Day Combo	4.99
Today's offering of deep-dish quiche served with a choice of soup of the day or garden salad.	
Mexican Club	5.99
A flour tortilla filled with turkey breast, bacon strips, lettuce, tomatoes and a Mexican style mayonnaise. Topped with cheddar cheese & finished in the oven.	

The final menu for Souper Salad restaurants (above) reflects the clients' preference for a bold cover design. Insert pages, however, follow the softer aqua-and-red color scheme that links the various arms of the company. Midnight Oil set up a template for the inserts using Aldus Pagemaker, so that the clients could easily make their own menu changes. As menu items come and go, new inserts can be copied or laser-printed onto pre-printed menu sheets.

Post-Industrial Stress & Design

Though a native of the Pacific Northwest, Skip Jensen had as a young man learned to ride the waves of southern California and Hawaii. He also learned the art of screen-printing surf-culture designs onto T-shirts. Eventually, Jensen established Fine Print Studios to create not only T-shirts, but also greeting cards and fine art serigraphs of up to forty colors.

When Jensen moved his printing business back to Tacoma, Washington, however, he discovered that another area printer was already using the Fine Print name. He brought the problem to Art Chantry, a Seattle graphic designer who had illustrated some T-shirts for him and had helped him get re-established on the mainland.

Chantry saw right away that Jensen's two businesses—T-shirts and fine art serigraphs—were not well delineated. In addition, Jensen was moving more in the direction of creating and selling bizarrely printed T-shirts. Clearly, the old "Fine Print" name needed to be changed to something that would better reflect the organiza-

tion of Jensen's company.

One of Chantry's personal fascinations had always been American industrial iconography of the 1940s and '50s—an imagery he had never seen anywhere else in American culture. Since Jensen's shop was in an old building in an industrial area of Tacoma, Chantry suggested using this visual language to create a pop image for Jensen's business.

Chantry also offered Jensen a name. At one time he had considered calling his own studio Post-Industrial Stress & Design, and he thought the name was ideally suited to Jensen's business. Jensen agreed—he liked both the name and the fact that it lent itself to interesting imagery.

Jensen's most pressing need was a name and identity to keep his commercial printing business running. From Post-Industrial Stress & Design, it was an easy leap to Post-Industrial Press, which Chantry saw as a division of the larger company. With Jensen's blessing, he set to work developing graphics in the spirit of the name.

Fine Print Studio's old imagery conveyed a mixed message—artful when applied to corporate stationery, but bizarre when applied to letterheads and price lists for Jensen's T-shirt business.

POST·INDUSTRIAL PRESS

Following his fascination with industrial images from the 1940s and '50s, Chantry drew upon clip art from that period to develop a mark for Post-Industrial Press. For the name itself, he created a hand-spaced modernistic logotype.

Chantry's logomark trials for Post-Industrial Press were created with black marker and a photocopier and faxed to Jensen for comment. Both designer and client preferred the same image (right, center), except that Jensen didn't like the boarded-up windows.

With the printing company's mark conceptually approved, Chantry focused on a coordinating image for the larger company. He toyed with different ideas, but the icon of a gear and the notion of stress kept coming to mind. His thumbnails (one of them is on the back of a credit card receipt) graphically convey those ideas.

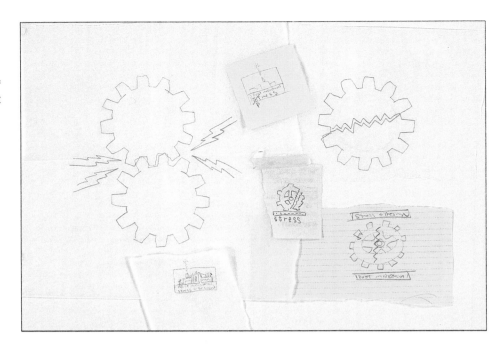

The final comped identities, as faxed to Skip Jensen. They received an instant okay.

To further glorify the industrial ver-
nacular, Chantry drew upon the
print-shop environment. Although
he had originally conceived both
logomarks in black and white, the
black-and-yellow safety tape Jensen used in his shop caught the
designer's eye. He worked up
some tissues for a stationery system combining the logomarks and
the striped tape as a linking motif.

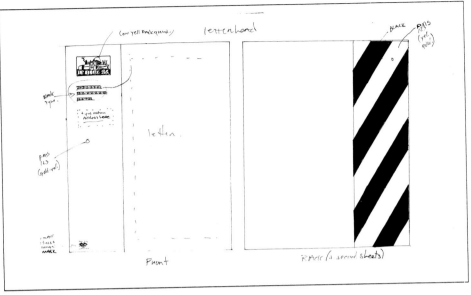

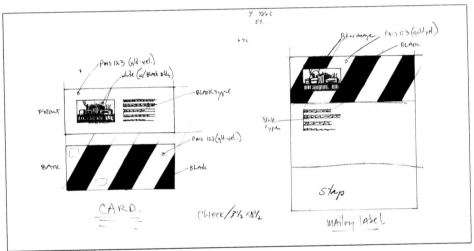

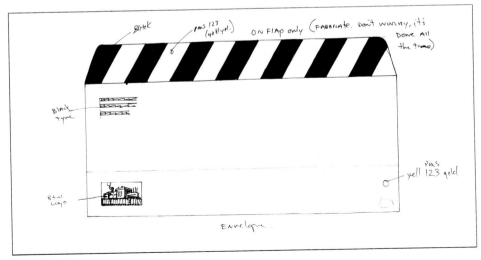

The new identity was implemented on business papers, calling cards, labels, hangtags, and a greeting card for Post-Industrial Press, a division of Post-Industrial Stress & Design. Note that the inside of the envelope and the flip-side of the letterhead have been imprinted with the safety-tape motif.

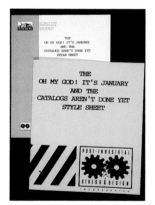

The identity was also applied to an interim Post-Industrial Press style sheet (above), a catalog, and the backs of some of the press' greeting cards (right).

Jensen silk-screened interior and exterior signage and continued the safety-tape look as a decorator touch.

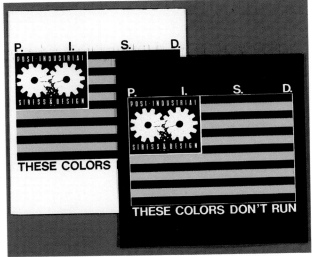

Since Jensen is himself an artist, he easily picked up Chantry's design and ran with it. Here, he's introduced the corporate identity as a T-shirt design . . .

. . . as well as an official Post-Industrial Press hard-hat and paddle-ball set.

Corporate identity programs, large and small. Morgan's/Morgan's Bistro, a downtown restaurant and its suburban branch (Katz Wheeler), page 118. Citybooks, a bookstore (Kiku Obata & Company), page 119. Educable, an educational cable TV station (Rickabaugh Graphics), page 120. South Side YMCA (Samata Associates), page 120. U.S. Canoe and Kayak Team, an Olympic team (Crosby Associates), page 121.

Financial Horizons, a subsidiary of Nationwide Insurance (Rickabaugh Graphics), page 122. Print Craft, printer for graphic designers (Charles S. Anderson Design Co.), page 123. Lithocolor, printer/engraver (Samata Associates), page 124. Robert Buzzeo, wood shingle manufacturer (Jack Hough Associates), page 125. Trinity Woodworks, custom cabinetry (Held & Diedrich Design), page 125. The Woodshop, handmade wooden furniture (Jon Flaming, Sullivan Perkins), page 125.

Mansion House, an upscale multiuse complex (Kiku Obata & Company), pages 126-127. Andrés Fotolab (Crosby Associates), page 128. Minneapolis College of Art and Design, a small art school (Charles S. Anderson Design Co.), page 129. Wok 'n' Roll, a Chinese carry-out (Held & Diedrich Design), page 130. Common Ground, a hospital's psychiatric center for troubled teens (Larson Design Associates), page 131.

Graphic Papers, a distributor of coated and textured printing papers (Taylor & Browning Design Associates), page 132. Bridlewood Residential Development (Held & Diedrich Design), page 133. The Landis Group/Tower Center, a real estate development company and its mixed-use complex (Cook & Shanosky Associates, Inc.), page 133. The Stamford Center for the Arts, (Jack Hough Associates, Inc.), pages 134-135.

Morgan's/Morgan's Bistro

Morgan's, a Philadelphia restaurant billing itself as a "delightful country inn in the heart of Center City," had approached the Philadelphia graphic design firm of Katz Wheeler with the need for a dual identity—one for the downtown restaurant itself, and one for its more informal suburban location. Katz Wheeler responded with an elegant, hand-drawn logotype clearly conveying the main eatery's casual elegance. For the suburban branch, the addition of the word "bistro," in a well-spaced sans serif face, clearly communicates that location's ambience. These separate flavors were then carried through in the respective menu designs. For downtown, lush pastel drawings executed in Katz Wheeler's own studio capture the light of the French countryside; for the more urbane bistro, which has highly changeable menus, the designers devised a format that could be easily redesigned every few weeks, using standardized type and varying pieces of found art.

Logomark for Morgan's (downtown location)

Logomark for Morgan's Bistro (suburban location)

Morgan's menus

Menus for Morgan's Bistro

Citybooks

When Citybooks opened in one of St. Louis' prosperous western suburbs, its owner wanted to make the shop the largest bookstore in all of Missouri. Located in a commercial center associated with good living, Citybooks offered a comprehensive collection of classic and contemporary titles, as well as an array of periodicals. Despite the granite and marble of its surroundings, the bookstore itself was eminently cozy, with hot coffee and comfortable armchairs encouraging browsing. In devising an identity for the shop, designers Kiku Obata & Company chose a look that combines both personality and elegance. They first fashioned a cityscape out of books, enclosing it in an Art Deco frame. Then they selected warm paper stocks and contemporary colors to execute a limited number of materials, aimed at giving the proprietor the greatest mileage possible from his identity investment. Beyond the basic stationery package, bookmarks are a favorite giveaway, and stickers and gift tags turn inexpensive commodity wraps into impressive gift packaging. On each item, judiciously applied silver foil-stamping adds just the right touch of elegance for Citybooks' upscale customers.

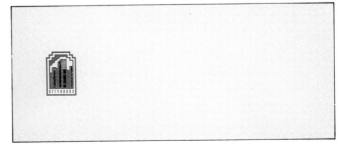

Shopping bag, gift wrap showing sticker, and bookmark

Stationery and gift tag

Educable

Educable, an educational cable TV station based in Columbus, Ohio, provides both subject-related and interactive programming for elementary and high school classes. But despite its local-station status, when the company first went on the air, it had to compete with both public broadcasting and larger, more powerful commercial channels in southern Ohio. The broadcasters obviously needed a graphic identity that would both represent the nature of their broadcasts and position the company as a serious contender in the Columbus market. Designed by Rickabaugh Graphics, also of Columbus, Educable's prime identifier takes the shape of an apple transformed into a TV screen; clean typography says "corporate" while lending an air of established credibility. A simple two-color production keeps restocking costs at a minimum.

South Side YMCA

In time of economic hardship, the YMCA of Metropolitan Chicago could not afford to keep all of its neighborhood centers open. Unfortunately, poorer neighborhoods — those most often in need of the Y's social programs — were often the first to go. The South Side Y, however, represents an inspiring counter to that trend. Housed in a brand new building near Hyde Park and the University of Chicago, this Y represented a renewed commitment to a troubled neighborhood, and its graphic identity needed to reflect that. Long associated with Chicago's Ys, Samata Associates, based in nearby Dundee, developed an identity system that brings a positive note to the project. With soaring rays emerging from a "Y" with outstretched arms, the new symbol presents an inspirational picture of growth and hope. This is amplified through the system's implementation in bright colors, across a range of informational, promotional and informal applications.

Stationery system

Stationery system

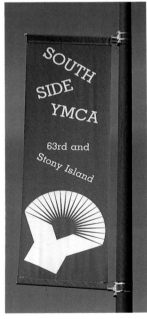

Banner

U.S. Canoe and Kayak Team

When Champion International became corporate sponsor of the U.S. Canoe and Kayak Team, the design-conscious forest-products company asked Chicago designers Crosby Associates to develop a new graphic identity for the team. To avoid the cumbersome complexity of the existing logomark, which tried to depict all of the activities included in this Olympic sport, the designers opted for a more abstract approach. Here, they focused on the spirit of the sport and attributes such as speed, flow and power or strength. Their solution includes a mixed-face logotype and a starlike symbol that suggests rapid, flowing waters and the bow of a canoe or kayak. A brief, three-panel standards "manual" provides repro materials and offers basic advice on application of the logomark.

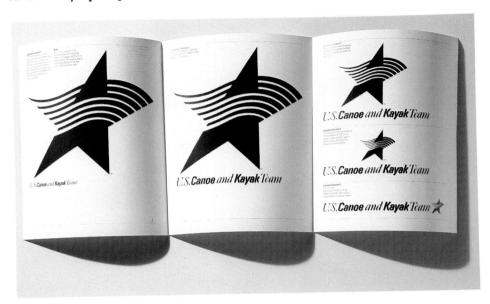

Standards "manual" for identity program

Team jackets

Financial Horizons

A subsidiary of Nationwide Insurance, Financial Horizons sells annuities and other insurance products through proprietary desks located in branch offices of various banks. The company's identity, therefore, had to appeal to two distinct audiences: the bank executives who let Financial Horizons set up shop in their lobbies, and individuals in the market for financial products. The graphics program devised by Rickabaugh Graphics of Columbus, Ohio, is conservative enough to appeal to the banking community, yet warm enough for the man in the street. While a symbol incorporating a rising sun suggests a company providing hope and security, traditional typestyles and soft-textured papers are decidedly low key. The new look was initially applied to basic stationery and a much-needed facilities brochure; a full-scale implementation is underway.

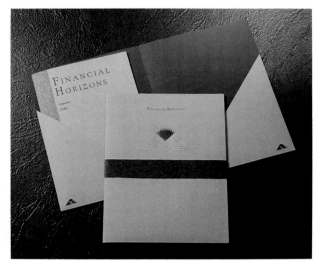

Identity system including stationery, facilities brochure, and other promotional materials

Application of the identity to both interior and exterior of brochure

Print Craft

When Print Craft, an industrial printer based in St. Paul, Minnesota, shifted to quality printing for graphic designers, Minneapolis designers at Charles S. Anderson Co. created a new graphic identity for it. Although the goal of the program was to suggest Print Craft's commitment to fine craftsmanship, the state-of-the-art solution, with its bold, black bars and gearlike symbol, also reflects the printer's industrial roots. At the same time, the identity offers a strong contrast to competitors' graphics, which stress four-color spectrums and rainbow imagery. While applications to business papers are purposefully understated, vehicle graphics—perhaps the most visible part of the program—are unmistakable.

Stationery system

Business forms

Promotional piece   Poster

Vehicle graphics

Lithocolor

Dundee, Illinois designers Samata Associates had been a longtime customer of the Chicago-based IPP Lithocolor when the engraver approached the firm about developing a new graphic identity. With the advent of new engraving technologies and a more competitive marketing environment, Lithocolor's existing identity appeared outdated and stodgy. To correct the situation, Samata Associates devised an identifier that better reflects the engraver's leading-edge technology and considerable technical expertise. The basic identifier is an "L" built out of engraver's dots, thus suggesting both Lithocolor's business and its complete control of the engraving process. To increase the program's visibility and also to have some fun, each of the company's various business papers was printed in an array of fluorescent colors that the engraver and its representatives could mix and match.

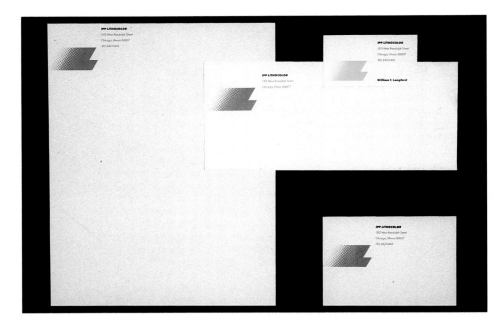

Stationery system

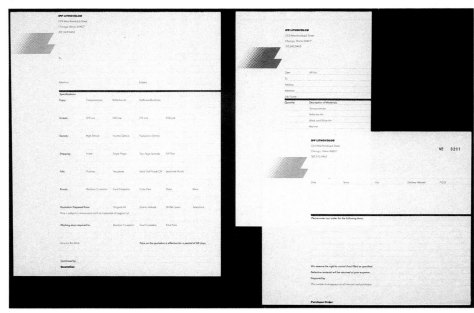

Business forms: invoice, delivery receipt, purchase order

Robert Buzzeo, Wood Shingle Manufacturer

Robert Buzzeo had a secret labor of love: making wooden shingles with old equipment he had repaired and refurbished himself. When he decided to turn his love into profits, he asked a customer—Jack Hough Associates, in Norwalk, Connecticut—to devise a graphic identity that would distinguish his new business from the many other small concerns in the area. Their recommendation was both clear and immediate: A series of solid "Bs," overlapping to suggest the shingles themselves. Woodsy colors and a moderately priced stock complete the economy-minded picture.

Trinity Woodworks

While the name of this custom cabinetry workshop reflects the strong religious ethic of its owners, its graphic identity conveys the care and traditional craftsmanship that goes into each handmade piece. Designed by Held & Diedrich Design in Indianapolis, Indiana, the program includes both stationery and a small brochure that explains Trinity's commitment to its craft. Rough papers in different colors, soft illustrations of hand tools, and the rich green and purple inks used to print them create immediate market credibility. At the same time, they suggest a system far more expensive than this one- and two-color production really is.

The Woodshop

When his father found he needed a business card to hand out at the flea markets and craft fairs where he sold his handmade wooden furniture, designer Jon Flaming designed a stationery package and printed it himself. Shaped like the blade of a circular saw, the symbol features a reversed logotype and the garage-cum-workshop where the elder Flaming works. Both the symbol and address copy were cast as rubber stamps for the utmost economy of reproduction.

Stationery and business card

Stationery, cover and inside spread of brochure

Stationery system and rubber stamps

Mansion House

Mansion House, an old apartment building in downtown St. Louis, had just been purchased by a developer who hoped to turn the aging landmark into an attractive, upscale, multiuse complex. Local designers Kiku Obata & Company were called in to spruce up the building's image. While other residential towers in the area had opted for a more austere image, the designers felt a warmer look would attract the desired commercial element and make more young professionals want to call Mansion House home. The resulting symbol clearly locates the building on the banks of the Mississippi; its component parts, including typography, rules and roses, are used separately to create collateral materials such as ads, promotions, even streetside banners.

Streetside banners

Sticker

Poster

Stationery, shopping bag and
complementary rose

Andrés Fotolab

The identity program for one of Chicago's premier photo labs clearly communicates *color*. Approached by Andrés Fotolab to develop a graphic identity within a modest budget, Crosby Associates created a basic system that the lab could further implement on its own. Because Crosby Associates was also one of Andrés' customers, the designers were quick to understand that the lab's delivery envelopes, as well as its delivery vehicles, formed the company's primary public interface.

Thus, the decision was made to keep the graphic design itself simple and colorful, so it would be recognized when seen anywhere. A custom logotype was reversed out of boldly colored letterheads, invoices, calling cards and envelopes; each component comes in a number of colors that the client can mix at will. The delivery wagons, like the large delivery envelopes themselves, are advertisements in motion as couriers make their stops around town.

Stationery system

Delivery vehicle graphics

Delivery envelopes

Minneapolis College of Art and Design

When this small art school split from the Minneapolis Institute of Arts, administrators asked the Charles S. Anderson Design Co., also of Minneapolis, to create a new graphic identity. To express MCAD's independent spirit and renewed dedication to art and design, the designers developed a complex image rife with symbolism: the school's well-known initials; a classically styled letter "M"; an eye toward the future; and a modernistic figure wielding a flaglike pencil. This design was then modified and adapted, in whole or in part, to a variety of items for sale in the college bookstore. With its postmodern underpinnings, the new look is at once traditional and contemporary, and provides the school with an interesting and changeable array of graphic elements for use through time.

Stationery system

Pencil box exterior

Pencil box interior

Chalk box

T-shirt

Wok 'n' Roll

Three brothers with experience as restaurateurs in Indianapolis wanted to open a Chinese carry-out with a difference: They wanted to attract an upscale crowd, and they wanted their new business experience to be *fun*. To help accomplish these objectives, they chose the unlikely name of Wok 'n' Roll and called in Indianapolis designers Held & Diedrich to translate it into graphics. Their "flying noodles" symbol and its confettilike surrounding motif immediately suggest that this is a Chinese restaurant like no other. While the graphics were applied with some restraint to business papers and menus, the designers saw in the ubiquitous carry-out containers a promotional opportunity not to be missed. For these commodity boxes and bags, the symbol and logo were printed on foil stickers that could be quickly affixed to each outgoing order. Finally, the look was expanded to include signage for the carry-out storefront, where a few tables had been arranged to accommodate patrons who prefer to eat in.

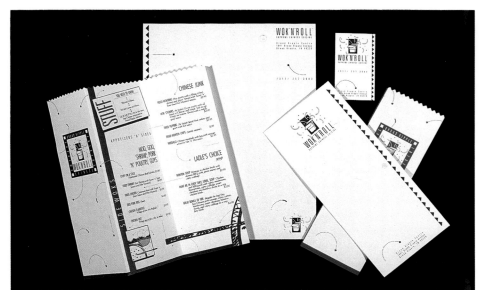

Stationery system and menus

Foil sticker for carry-out bags and boxes

Common Ground

Sometimes an organization with a comprehensive graphic identity has a component that needs to be graphically set apart. Such was the case at the Stamford Hospital in Stamford, Connecticut, where Larson Design Associates, of Rockford, Illinois, had just completed an identity overhaul. The unit in question was the hospital's psychiatric center for troubled teens. Hospital administrators hoped that a unique identity would make the center less threatening to teens and their parents, and encourage referrals from social service agencies within the community. Larson Design first developed a name, Common Ground, to suggest the program's philosophical base, then set about developing a graphic identity. The heart of the system is a pair of interlocking profiles that represent parents and teenagers coming together to discuss their problems. To reflect Common Ground's own parentage, Larson developed the unit's identity within the grid devised for the Stamford Hospital.

Stationery system

Interior and front cover of brochure

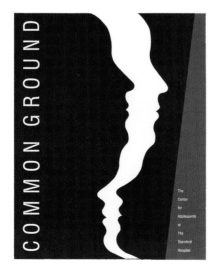

Press folder

Graphic Papers

Based in Toronto, Ontario, Graphic Papers is a major distributor of fine-quality coated and textured printing papers. It was imperative, therefore, that the company's graphic identity be of the highest caliber, so as to appeal to printing industry professionals and graphic designers alike. The identity system devised by Toronto's Taylor & Browning Design Associates is all of that, and more. Its primary symbol captures the feel of both product and selection and is adaptable to a number of applications. The palette is clear and basic, using white space as a color in its own right. Beyond stationery and other business papers, the identity has been extended to sample boxes and swatch books, price lists, advertising, packaging, signage and vehicles.

Brand logos for various papers

Identity system including stationery, business forms, boxes and mugs

Vehicle graphics

Bridlewood Residential Development

Designed by Indianapolis' Held & Diedrich Design, the graphic identity for the Bridlewood residential development near Zionsville, Indiana, takes inspiration from nearby horse-boarding stables. Despite its low-budget production, the use of a rich green and tan color palette creates a classic country charm especially geared to appeal to the development's upscale target market. The identity was also applied to a simple brochure and a luncheon announcement sent to builders and other developers, inviting them to participate in creating Bridlewood.

The Landis Group/Tower Center

Real estate developer Alan Landis was involved in a number of projects in the Princeton, New Jersey/Philadelphia, Pennsylvania corridor. At one of these sites, designers Cook & Shanosky Associates, Inc. were asked by the architects to design environmental graphics. Impressed with their expertise, Landis himself then retained the designers directly to develop graphic identities for several of his properties. Among these was Tower Center, a mixed-use complex in East Brunswick, New Jersey. Composed of twin office towers linked by a Ramada Renaissance Hotel, the multi-use nature of this complex is expressed with a symbol drawn from the tower forms and stamped in silver on a textured buff stock. As Landis's projects continued to multiply, he came to see his business in a new light. Accordingly, he asked Cook and Shanosky to develop a totally separate look to reflect the newly restructured Landis Group. Devised with clean lines and strong, clear colors, this symbol is built from staggered "Ls" and suggests both architectural forms and a multiplicity of development projects.

Bridlewood stationery and collateral

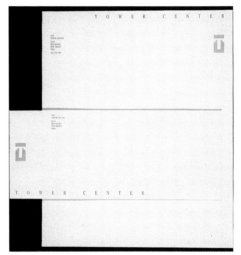

Tower Center stationery system

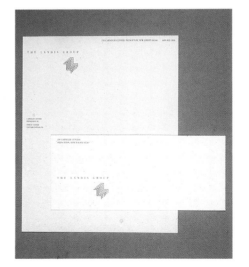

The Landis Group stationery

Stamford Center for the Arts

Filled with the prospect of building an exciting new performance space, the Stamford (Connecticut) Center for the Arts asked Norwalk designers Jack Hough Associates, Inc. to develop a graphic identity that could take the performing arts organization to the fundraising kickoff and beyond. The designers responded with a simple yet visually exciting system revolving around four cleanly drawn but differently patterned stars. The stars were printed in varying colors across a range of business papers and adapted to newspaper ads and program mailers. Besides representing the various types of performances the center offered, the design also reflected the stellar quality of its world-class guest artists. Moreover, the polished, almost corporate approach to the design was especially appropriate, given the center's primary fundraising targets: the many corporations headquartered in Stamford and affluent Fairfield County.

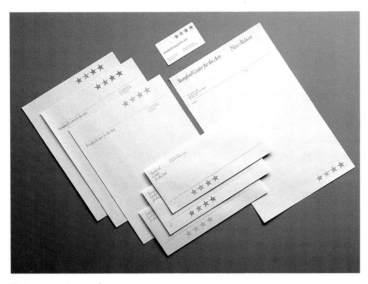

Stationery system and news release

Collateral

Black-and-white ads

Stamford Center for the Arts

The Nutcracker

Performed by the Connecticut Ballet
with the Chamber Orchestra of New England

| Wed, Th, Fri | Dec. 21–23 | 8pm | $16, 14, 10 |
| Th, Fri, Sat | Dec. 22–24 | 2pm | $13, 11, 7 |

307 Atlantic Street, Stamford CT 06901
(Corner, Tresser Blvd.) Call 323-2131

VISA/MasterCard
Group rates avail.

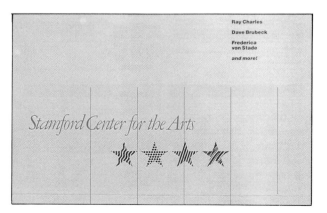

Ray Charles

Dave Brubeck

Frederica
von Stade

and more!

Stamford Center for the Arts

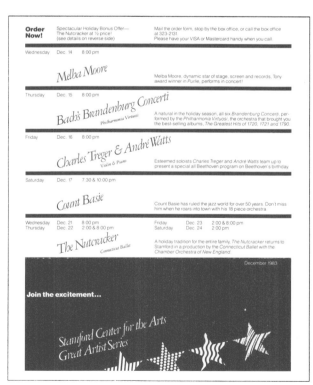

Order Now!

Spectacular Holiday Bonus Offer—
The Nutcracker at ½ price!
(see details on reverse side)

Mail the order form, stop by the box office, or call the box office at 323-2131.
Please have your VISA or Mastercard handy when you call.

Wednesday   Dec. 14   8:00 pm

Melba Moore

Melba Moore, dynamic star of stage, screen and records, Tony award winner in *Purlie*, performs in concert!

Thursday   Dec. 15   8:00 pm

Bach's Brandenburg Concerti
Philharmonia Virtuosi

A natural in the holiday season, all six *Brandenburg Concerti*, performed by the *Philharmonia Virtuosi*, the orchestra that brought you the best-selling albums, *The Greatest Hits of 1720, 1721 and 1790*.

Friday   Dec. 16   8:00 pm

Charles Treger & André Watts
Violin & Piano

Esteemed soloists *Charles Treger* and *André Watts* team up to present a special all Beethoven program on Beethoven's birthday.

Saturday   Dec. 17   7:30 & 10:00 pm

Count Basie

Count Basie has ruled the jazz world for over 50 years. Don't miss him when he roars into town with his 18 piece orchestra.

| Wednesday | Dec. 21 | 8:00 pm | Friday | Dec. 23 | 2:00 & 8:00 pm |
| Thursday | Dec. 22 | 2:00 & 8:00 pm | Saturday | Dec. 24 | 2:00 pm |

The Nutcracker
Connecticut Ballet

A holiday tradition for the entire family, *The Nutcracker* returns to Stamford in a production by the *Connecticut Ballet* with the *Chamber Orchestra of New England*.

December 1983

Join the excitement...

*Stamford Center for the Arts
Great Artist Series*

Index